USA TODA

TRACKING TOMORROW'S TRENDS

What We Think About Our Lives and Our Future

Anthony M. Casale
with Philip Lerman

Andrews, McMeel & Parker
A Universal Press Syndicate Affiliate
Kansas City • New York

Library of Congress Cataloging-in-Publication Data

Casale, Anthony.
　　Tracking tomorrow's trends.

　　1. United States—Population.　2. United States—
Economic conditions—1981-　　.　3. United States—
Social conditions—1980-　　.　4. United States—
Social life and customs—1971-　　.　I. Lerman,
Philip.　II. Title.
HB3505.C37　1986　　304.6'0973　　86-20607
ISBN 0-8362-7934-4

Thanks . . .

To Phil Lerman, my friend in Washington who helped edit my thoughts and without whom this book wouldn't have been possible—at least not on time. And to Donna Martin, who edited the results.

To Nancy Woodhull, my boss, colleague, and my friend for more than a decade, who taught me that just good enough is not good enough.

To Dr. Gordon S. Black, who taught me so much about research.

To Al Neuharth, John Quinn, John Curley, and my other Gannett colleagues who made possible USA TODAY and everything that followed.

And most of all, to my family, Debbie, Tom, and Amy who had the toughest job of all: They had to live with me while I wrote this book.

TONY CASALE

CONTENTS

PREFACE

A poll is like a snapshot in time, a freeze-frame photograph of what we think, love, feel, and fear about our lives. Put a lot of these snapshots together and they turn into a motion picture. What we've done here is to run that motion picture backward and forward; to take a look at life in the USA today, and what it might be like tomorrow.

The data on which this book is based came from more than 100 public opinion polls which the author directed for USA TODAY over the past 10 years. In all, more than 100,000 people were surveyed.

Surveys, even the best, contain a margin of error. We caution you about this, but assure you that each poll was conducted according to the very highest standards of survey research.

We can say one thing with absolute certainty: This is your book, not ours. It is the voice of the USA, a compilation of things you told us about yourselves, and our nation.

Some of what you told us has been contradictory, some of it has been confusing. Some of it has been disappointing, but more, much more, has been hopeful and optimistic.

We need to thank all the editors and reporters who worked with us over the years at USA TODAY. Most of all, however, we want to thank you.

CHAPTER ONE

Who We Are

Meet Robert. Meet Linda.

Robert is pushing 31. He wakes up in the morning after sleeping 7 hours and 57 minutes, and commutes 21 minutes to a job that's paying him $25,861 a year. His favorite color is blue; he wears a 40 regular suit. He weighs 173 and has a 34-inch waist, not bad for his height, which is just over 5-foot-8.

Linda got about nine minutes more sleep last night than Robert did. She's two years and four months older and stands about four inches shorter. She's making $16,030 a year.

There they are. Mr. and Ms. '80s USA.

Robert's stats are the average statistics for a male in the USA today. Linda's are the average statistics for a woman. In fact, Robert and Linda were the most popular names for babies born at the same time as our average man and woman. (In 1986 the favorite names were Michael and Jennifer.)

In a way, this is a book about them—the average man and woman. What they think. How they live. How they will change in the years ahead.

A lot has been written about this decade, enough to make you feel that nobody knows what's going on. For every guy in a blow-dry haircut on TV telling you that the USA is returning to the traditional values of the '50s there's some newspaper article telling you that some new age is dawning (the computer age, the video age, the age of divorce, the AIDS age, the age of the working mother).

We hear that the traditional family is returning, though the divorce rate is somewhere near the national debt.

So who are the people of the USA? And where are they going? What are they like now? And what will they be like in the '90s? How can you profit from the changes taking place? Prepare for them?

We wondered about it. So we went to the source.

We asked you.

We asked a lot of important questions and a whole lot of nosy ones. And we got some fascinating answers in our effort to track tomorrow's trends.

Yes, there are "traditional" values, if you want to call them that, and we are building on them as we speed into the '90s. There are also some very startling findings. The changes that our country has lived through in the last few decades haven't caused us to discard our values. They are being incorporated into a national lifestyle that brings together some good and some bad parts of different lifestyles that have gone before it.

Take women, for example. What they told us is:

- Yes, they have fought successfully for their share of the workplace and they will continue to make strides in the '90s. This is very important to them.
- But no, they're not at all willing to give up the job of being a good mother and homemaker.

Now, trying to live up to all that is sort of like trying to be Superwoman. It can drive you a little crazy. But most women tell us they're not about to give up either of their roles.

Or take college kids. Think they've become as conservative as the bobby-soxers? Wait till you hear what they say about sex and drinking.

But more than anything else, what we discovered when we listened to the USA speak was this: The '80s are a time of diversity, of conflict, and of hope. They are a confusing time for many of us. And, for many of us a time where more than anything else we're striving to get and keep more control of our lives. There's a good chance many of us can achieve that goal in the years ahead.

We found a lot of Robert and Linda in the answers—and a lot of answers that made Robert and Linda seem like silly concepts. We found one nation and a thousand nations, a people united and diverse. We found some things that seem to be common themes, and heard some things that were uncommonly confusing.

So before we head into that multicolored painting of the USA, let's lay down a base coat. In this first chapter, we'll present the facts—some very important, some less important—about the USA's people.

Then we'll listen to what they have to say about life in the '80s and beyond.

Counting Noses

Starting then with the basics: There are 237 million of us who share the distinction of being citizens of the USA. Most of us—about 236.2 million—actually live in the USA.

In 1970, there were only 204.4 million of us, and in 1980 a mere 227 million. But then again, we're not a nation that stands still.

You wouldn't know it from looking at our cities, but there's actually a lot of room here in the USA. An average of 66.7 people occupy each square mile, or about 422,400 square feet for every man, woman, and child.

When we do cluster together, we pick places like Washington D.C., or that famous "city that never sleeps," Jersey City.

Jersey City? That's right—the most densely populated city in the nation is not New York City but just across the Hudson in Jersey City, N.J., where an average of 12,000 people live in every square mile.

The District of Columbia has more residents per square mile (9,886, to be precise) than any of the 50 states.

If you're looking for your fair share of space, check out Alaska, where you could get a square mile to yourself if you didn't mind snow on it.

The five most densely populated states (not counting D.C.):

	People per square mile
New Jersey	1,006
Rhode Island	912
Massachusetts	741

Connecticut	647
Maryland	442

The five least populated states:

	People per square mile
Alaska	1
Wyoming	5
Montana	6
Nevada	8
South Dakota	9

That's About the Size of It

We never did finish telling you about Robert and Linda, the average man and woman in the USA. On the average. . .

Here's how men spend the day:

Eating:	1 hour, 20 minutes
Personal care:	65 minutes
Commuting	42 minutes
Sleeping	7 hours, 57 minutes
Working	6 hours, 17 minutes

The average man:

Height	5 feet, 8 inches
Waist size	34 inches
Weight	173 pounds
Income	$25,861
Suit size	40 regular

Here's how women spend the day:

Eating:	1 hour, 13 minutes
Personal care	1 hour, 17 minutes
Commuting	30 minutes
Sleeping	8 hours, 6 minutes
Work	5 hours, 4 minutes

The average woman:

Height	5 feet, 4 inches
Weight	142 pounds

Income	$16,030
Dress size	12

And while we're on the subject of What We Do All Day:
- On an average day, 70 percent of us take a shower and 27 percent take a bath; 62 percent drink coffee and 16 percent will drink a beer; 36 percent skip breakfast; 18 percent wear jogging shoes for street wear.
- The average person on an average day will drink an average of 1.54 cups of coffee.
- The average man on a 1,500- to 1,600-calorie-a-day diet will lose one to two pounds a week. Most women must eat no more than 1,000 to 1,200 calories a day to lose one to two pounds a week.

Out of every 1,000 of us in the USA, here's what will happen this year:
- Nine will die
- Eleven will get married.
- Five will get divorced (and most will be happy about it, as we'll see in a few chapters).
- Six will be the victim of a violent crime of some kind; 76 will be the victim of a theft; and 71 will be the victim of a robbery.

Money

There are many ways to look at money (longingly is the first that comes to mind), but no matter how you look at it we are among the richest people on earth.

About 13 percent of all households have incomes of more than $50,000. More than 4.4 million of us have assets over $300,000 including at least 407,700 millionaires. That's twice the number from the beginning of the decade, so clearly the '80s have been easier for some people than for others.

Women, by the way, haven't done all that badly: The number of wealthy women increased 200 percent in the first half of this decade.

Those of us who aren't rich often dream of getting that way. People in the USA buy $12 billion in lottery tickets each year. Unfortunately, they win only $5.8 billion, which may be why it's called dreaming.

If you're looking for rich people, here are the best states to look in: California, Texas, and New York. The states with the fewest rich people are Vermont, Rhode Island, and Delaware.

Yet, despite our affluence, 21 percent of all households have total incomes of less than $10,000. And about 7.3 million families—almost 12 percent—live in poverty.

Them That's Got

Disposable income was about $10,887 in the mid-'80s, compared with about $3,400 in 1970 and $8,032 in 1980. This is the money that we have left to spend on things we want after all the necessities such as food and the rent are paid.

The median family income was $26,433. That breaks down to an average of $27,686 for white families and $15,432 for blacks.

How much money do we think we need to live comfortably? That answer depends on how much you already have. The more we've got the more we want.

People making less than $15,000 say they need about $26,000 to live comfortably. People making $26,000 say they need about $34,000.

How Old Are You Now?

As a nation, we are accomplishing a neat feat: growing older and younger at the same time.

How do we do it? Aside from the fact that this is the USA where anything is possible, there's really a simple explanation.

First, the younger part. You've heard of the "baby boom"— all those kids born roughly between the time the Allies landed at Normandy and the Beatles landed at JFK airport. Well, they're old enough to have kids of their own now—and that's exactly what they're doing.

The result of this "baby boom echo": The number of kids under age five soared almost 9 percent during the first half of the '80s, and is expected to continue growing.

OK, now for the flip side: We are also a nation growing older.

The median age is 31.3 years—up from 28 in the 1970s. People age 65 and older make up 11.9 percent of the USA's population, an increase of almost 10 percent just during the first half of the 1980s. By the year 2050, one in five of us will be 65 or older.

These are not just statistical trivialities. Both of these trends will have an enormous impact on society as we move into the '90s and beyond. We'll talk about this more in later chapters—but just for starters. What are we going to do with all those young kids?

For years, school districts across the nation have been closing and selling school buildings because of declining enrollment. Now, they will be forced to reverse this trend and find someplace to put this new influx of young children.

Already, kindergartens are beginning to feel the pinch—like someone buying tighter jeans after going on a diet and then gaining a few pounds. This is only the beginning. A decade from now your local newspaper will be writing stories about the same problems in the junior high school. The strain on school and child-care facilities will continue to grow through the end of the century.

And the real "generation gap" these days is between the ages of five and 17—too young for the baby boom, too old for the echo boom. There are simply fewer people of that age these days.

For people in this "generation gap," it will mean better job prospects because there is less competition. If you're the manager of a fast food restaurant, however, you've got your work cut out for you. Expect to spend a few years scrambling for help, since the pool of workers is going to keep shrinking until all those kindergarteners become old enough to flip a burger.

As for the older people—the USA will suddenly realize how many of them there are, and how much money they have and what a tempting market they are. In fact, the "mature market" is going to be one of the important phenomena of the '90s. By the way, Florida is still their favorite spot—but other states are starting to vie successfully for the retirement dollar. We'll see later who's coming up strong—but here's the current status of Where We're Old:

States where the percentage of elderly is highest:

State	Percent of Population
Florida	17.6%
Arkansas	14.3
Rhode Island	14.3
Pennsylvania	14.1
Iowa	14.1

Because of the differences in lifespans, you'll find a lot more widows than widowers in those states: 74 percent of all men over 65 are married compared with only 36 percent of all women.

Knock on Any Door

Ward, I'm worried about the Beaver. He doesn't seem himself these days. In fact, sometimes I feel he's not all there.

Well, if you knock on the door of the typical family, you'll find that he's not. The average family in the USA has shrunk in size these days; it figures out to about one Ward Cleaver, one June Cleaver, a Wally, and about two-tenths of a Beaver.

The number of families fitting the "traditional" formula— a father who works, a mother who stays home, and two children—is shrinking drastically. Putting aside the issue of working mothers for a moment, the average size of the USA's 62 million families is 3.2 people.

Translating that into reality, it means that there are tens of thousands of married couples in the USA who have no children, and tens of thousands of other couples who have fewer children than their parents did.

Now throw the rest of the USA into the mix—single people, people with roommates, POSSLQs (Persons of Opposite Sex Sharing Living Quarters, pronounced "possel-cues," thanks to the Census Bureau). You wind up with a grand total of 87 million households in the USA, 7 percent more than in 1980.

If you knocked on all 87 million of those doors, you'd find an average of fewer than three people behind each one—2.71 people, to be exact. Behind every fourth door you would find someone living alone.

Here's an interesting milestone of our illustrious decade: We have left behind, probably forever, the days when it was likely that a married woman with small children would be a full-time homemaker.

It's not clear exactly when we passed the barrier—and history will never know the name of the woman who got the job that threw the statistic over the 50 percent mark. But today, 52 percent of married women with children under the age of six work.

What this means for the future—for relationships, for the workplace, for children, for the economy—could fill a book by itself. We'll come back to this subject. For now, let's just say it's a safe bet that issues of day care, maternity leave, and comparable worth will be key issues for companies to deal with in the '90s.

Also on the increase is the "To-hell-with-You-Ward-I'll-Deal-with-the-Beaver-Myself" factor. The number of families headed by women is soaring. In fact, over the past four years, nearly half of the 2.4 million *new* households were headed by women. All in all, 81 percent of families are headed by a married couple living together. Sixteen percent are headed by a woman without a man in the house.

There are some intriguing contrasts between men and women when it comes to how they're living and who they're living with. For example, here's how men stack up:

- 26 percent of all adult men are single, compared with 19 percent in 1970.
- 66 percent of men are married compared with 75 percent in 1970.
- 6 percent are divorced, double the 1970 figure.

Now here are the same figures for women:

- 19 percent are single. In 1970 it was 14 percent.
- 61 percent are married, compared with 69 percent then.
- 8 percent are divorced, compared with only 4 percent in 1970.

Most of the rest of these two groups are widows or widowers.

Men are more likely to marry after they have a divorce and they're more likely to marry younger women.

Take Two Giant Steps Forward

Two other giant steps women have taken in the '80s:
- For the first time, more women vote than men.
- For the first time in the USA's history, white males make up less than half of the working population.

Those are important turning points. On the work side, women accounted for 59 percent of the growth in the labor force during the late 1970s and the first half of the '80s. Overall, 53 percent of all women are in the labor force, including 63 percent of the single (never married) women and 75 percent of all divorcees.

In the voting booth, women have gained steadily. Here are the figures:

	Percentage of men voting	Percentage of women voting
1972	64.1	62.0
1976	59.6	58.8
1980	59.1	59.4
1984	59.0	60.8

Time Out for Some Other Facts

- We're writing more letters than we used to: 131.5 million in 1985, up from 119.4 million in 1983. Women are almost three times as likely as men to write letters.
- Gardening is a favorite leisure activity of 47 percent of the USA.
- 47 percent of us never use seat belts.
- We ate 175.7 pounds of meat per person in 1984.
- Walking, swimming, and fishing are more popular outdoor activities than jogging, tennis, and golf.

Nursery Rhymes and Reasons

Let's go back to the beginning. All the way back.

About 16 out of every 1,000 women will give birth this year.

Across the nation, women 18 to 24 can expect to give birth about twice in their lives.

But there are a lot of variables. Race is one, for example.

The birth rate for black women is 21 per 1,000; for white women, 15 per 1,000. Where you live is another. In 33 states, the average woman has fewer than two children in her lifetime. In Utah, possibly as a result of the strong influence of the Mormon church, the average is up around 3.2 children. In Massachusetts, Rhode Island, and Connecticut, it's about 1.5 children to a customer.

There is a critical demographic trend taking shape, however. The number of couples becoming parents for the first time is rising sharply. What does that mean? Well, a lot of people have delayed having children, and are just getting around to having their first. Those that haven't delayed are having their first child right on schedule. It's sort of like an elevator, with a lot of people getting on at a normal rate and another bunch rushing through just before the door closes.

One reason for fewer births overall, and for the delay in first-births, is fairly simple: We're getting married later. The median age (first marriages only, now) is 25 for men, 23 for women. This is causing a shift toward later childbearing—22 percent of the births in the mid-'80s were to women 30 and older, compared with 18 percent in 1970.

OK, so all that means that a lot of people are just now getting around to having their first child. There were 30.5 million families with children at home in 1980. This will increase steadily through the rest of the decade, the highest rate of first-time parents since just after World War II.

To whom is this trend of any importance? First and foremost to people who sell things for babies.

First-time parents are rabid spenders—they want to buy *everything*. People who have a child or two have lots of things like baby strollers and clothes left over.

Less pleased about this trend will be those businesses that know all too well that when people have a child they go out less and travel less.

Now, here's another interesting fact about The Beginning of All of This, which is tied by a short umbilical cord to a business concern. More than one in five women will give birth through Caesarean section, a rate up dramatically from a decade ago. The fact that more women are giving birth in their mid-to-late 30s may be one factor. The major reason, however, according to doctors: the high insurance rates for doctors and the fear of a lawsuit should something go wrong in childbirth.

OK, kid, so it took you awhile, and you may have come by Caesarean, but here you are. Guess what? You're more likely to be a boy than a girl. People always get this backward, since women grownups outnumber men grownups. But it's true: There are 105 males born for every 100 females. By the age of 25, women outnumber men 100 to 97, and the gap widens after that.

Finally, here's some good news for all of you kids being born today. You boys can expect to live to 71; and make that 78 for you girls.

School Days

Of course, kids are going to spend a good chunk of the first part of those 71 or 78 years in school. And they're going to wind up smarter than the generation before them.

We're becoming a more educated society. Already, 86 percent of all young adults, those under 34, have a high school diploma. And more than one out of four adults attended college.

And if you're a college student, the chances are better than 50-50 that you're a woman.

As in the workplace, women are making the greatest strides in the area of education.

What happened is this: College enrollment of women between the ages of 25 to 34 more than tripled during the '70s and early '80s. In 1970, 55 percent of incoming freshmen were men. It's now 48 percent male and 52 percent female.

We will pay $240 billion to educate our children through the 12th grade, up sharply during the '80s and expected to increase further even though the size of the school enrollment has stayed relatively stable since 1980.

The District of Columbia has the most highly educated population in the USA—28 percent have finished college. The national average is 16.3 percent. The lowest: Arkansas.

What's the quality of that education? This will be one of the USA's hottest debates as we move into the 1990s.

Several strong surveys have shown that teachers are leaving the profession—and all across the USA school districts are suffering from a growing teacher shortage that could reach epidemic proportions in the '90s if unchecked. One southern school district began running ads during spring break—imploring vacationing college students to stay there and become teachers.

Why is there a growing teacher shortage? Even though the average salary has risen to just under $24,000 (up from $9,300 in 1970), the main reason teachers give for leaving the profession—and experts feel students aren't entering it—is money. Teaching simply isn't financially competitive with other positions available to college graduates.

Go West (or South), Young Man

Imagine that the population of the continental U.S. is standing on a thin metal silhouette of the country a few feet above the ground and every person is of equal weight.

To keep the USA aloft you attach one end of a string to a gigantic helicopter and the other end to a balance point at the exact geographic center of the country; say, somewhere in Kansas.

Well, that won't work. There are more people in the East than in the West so the sheet begins to topple.

Try again. This time, attach it to some point in the middle of the *population* of the country—so there are an equal number of people on all sides.

I'll never be able to figure that out, you say! Fortunately, the U.S. Census Bureau has done it for us.

Back in 1790, that perfect midpoint was just east of Baltimore, Md. By the year 1900, it was six miles southeast of Columbus, Ohio. In 1960 it was outside Centralia, Ill. By 1980 the midpoint had moved south and west to De Soto, Mo.

Before we set the country back down again, let's speculate on where that imaginary center will be in 1990. Unfortunately, the folks over at Census haven't figured that one out yet, but we're betting that it will be at least 100 miles to the southwest of De Soto.

The reason for the shift in the days of Washington and Jefferson was Manifest Destiny, the urgent push to make the country stretch from sea to shining sea. The reason for the shift these days is Sun Belt Mania, the urgent push to live in a place where you spend less money on heating fuel and where you can get a tan while you walk to work.

The South and the West accounted for 92 percent of all growth in the early '80s. In 1970, one out of four men, women, and children lived in the Northeast. By the mid-'80s this had dropped to about one in five. In 1970, 28 percent lived in the Midwest; by 1985 this had dropped to 25 percent, a loss of 7 million people.

People were moving away, for all sorts of reasons. The recession of the late '70s and early '80s hit hard at states that were heavily reliant on industry. High fuel prices made it tougher to run a business. The high maintenance cost of a "Rust Belt" city, as the northeast quarter of the country came to be known, meant higher taxes. And as businesses moved South and West, cities there flourished—with new jobs and fresh, renovated downtowns to lure more people away from the Northeast.

As a result, 34 percent of the people in the USA now live in the South, up from 31 percent in 1970; and 20 percent live in the West, up from 17 percent in 1970—and that includes an increase of 2.4 million people through 1985 alone.

The fastest-growing county in the USA is Georgia's Gwinnett County, according to Dun & Bradstreet. It grew 50 percent since 1980—its population soaring from 166,903 to 251,025.

The Northeast and Midwest are showing some signs of a comeback. After several years of population loss, the hardest hit of the "Rust Belt" states, Ohio, Indiana, Illinois, and Michigan, showed gains in the 'mid-80s.

The trail of people moving out—which hit its stride following the recession of the early '80s—slowed as automakers and other industries recovered. Moreover, the pendulum shifted—such oil-rich states as Texas and Oklahoma were stunned by a slowdown in the petroleum industry and began to lose their luster for job-seekers.

Nevertheless, all of this amounts to a slowing, not a reversing, of the pattern: The country will continue to tilt down-and-to-the-left. Nearly 80 percent of the USA's growth by the year 2000 will occur in the South and West, according to the National Planning Association. California will be the biggest gainer, adding 6.7 million people.

**The big winners
(Expected gains by the year 2000)**

State	Growth in millions
California	6.7
Florida	5.8
Texas	5.7
Arizona	1.9
North Carolina	1.7

And if you look at the urban areas expected to be the fastest-growing for the rest of this century, you'll find they're all in the South and the West. Here are the top five:

1. West Palm Beach/Boca Raton, Fla.	61.3%
2. Phoenix, Ariz.	54.6
3. Orlando, Fla.	50.6
4. Riverside-San Bernardino, Calif.	41.8
5. Salt Lake City, Utah	35.5

And while we're on the subject of where people are moving from and where they're moving to—you can forget about most of what you've read about people returning to the cities. That all started with the oil embargo and high gas prices in the early '70s. But to an immense degree people are still parading to the suburbs, and have changed forever what this country looks like.

The numbers: In 1950, 35 million of us lived in the suburbs. That became 75 million in 1970 and 99 million in 1980.

Clearly the suburbs now dominate; 44 percent of us live there; 32 percent live in the cities and 24 percent in rural areas.

Some of this growth is spawning "Superburbs"—sprawling suburban city-ettes: hybrids of shopping centers, apartment complexes so big they seem like a neighborhood, condominiums, and more shopping centers.

Time out for Some More Facts

Oregon produces more particleboard than any other state. Virginia leads in explosives. Michigan is No. 1 in breakfast cereal. North Carolina makes more power tools. Missouri tops the nation with hats and caps.

Of the USA's 34,071 liquor stores, New Hampshire's state-run stores have the highest average sales. Privately owned stores in Kansas averaged the least.

Indiana is at the top of the scale in musical instrument manufacturing. Alabama is the leader in inner tubes.

Still a Melting Pot

The achievements of the USA's blacks in the last few decades have been greatly documented. But two other minority groups have made great strides—in different ways—through this decade.

Asian-Americans are the USA's fastest-growing minority group, and the rapidity with which they are entering society is matched only by their success in dealing with it.

They outperform all other population groups in the class-room and in the workplace, according to the Population Reference Bureau.

About 5.5 million Asians live in the USA—that's up from fewer than 1 million in 1960. Chinese and Filipinos make up the largest group of Asian-Americans. Overall, Asians now make up less than 3 percent of the population, but at the current rate they will number 10 million by the year 2000. That will still put them third in total numbers, behind blacks and Hispanics.

Yet Asians have a higher proportion of men finishing high school than do whites. They are also about twice as likely to have college degrees. Filipinos, Japanese, and Asian Indians are achieving particular success.

Hispanics are also gaining in the '80s.

The Census Bureau estimates there were 16.9 million Hispanics in the USA in 1985. The Hispanic population has grown five times as fast as the nation's total population.

Hispanics are on the average younger, less educated, have larger families and are more likely to be living in poverty than the typical USA population. They earned an average of $18,800 last year compared with $27,000 for others.

Hispanics have made strong political gains, however, in many areas of the country—most recently electing a Cuban mayor in Miami, where it is estimated that two out of three people speak a language other than English at home.

In fact, the number of Hispanic officials across the USA doubled from 1974 to 1984, even though a majority of the Latino population is not eligible to vote. An estimated 40 percent are under 18 years old, and many of voting age are ineligible because they're not citizens.

The political strength of Hispanics has caused some backlash and anger—partly visible in an "English-only" drive in 10 states, aimed at getting rid of bilingual signs and ballots in areas where there are large Hispanic populations. Hispanic officials say this push is motivated by racism.

English is not the primary language for about 23 million people. Almost half of these, 11 million, speak Spanish.

Also spoken here:

Language	Persons speaking
Italian	1.8 million
German	1.6 million
French	1.6 million
Polish	820,647
Chinese	630,000

Down on the Farm

The 1980s saw the worst farm crisis in perhaps half a century. At this writing tens of thousands of farmers face imminent foreclosure. Farmers and banks are playing out a tense waiting game that has focused the nation's attention on the plight of the farmer.

Oddly, the number of small farms actually grew during the first half of this decade. One reason behind this was "hobby farming," those farms being run by people who make their money elsewhere and farm for a hobby. Many of these are cropping up outside major urban areas.

Despite the increase in farms of less than 50 acres, the number of farms overall declined by more than 20,000 during the '80s.

In fact, less than half of all agricultural workers lived on farms in 1982. Only 34 cents of each food dollar spent went directly to farmers. Farmers received only 8 cents for a head of lettuce sold; 9 cents for the wheat in a loaf of bread; 58 cents a pound for beef; and 64 cents for a dozen eggs.

Health

To keep ourselves healthy, we will spend about $387.4 billion this year. That's approximately $1,580 for every man, woman, and child. Compare this to the U.S. budget deficit of about $200 billion.

About 41 percent of this, almost $160 billion, will go to hospitals; 20 percent, or $75 billion, will go to pay doctors.

The most freqently performed surgery in the nation for women is hysterectomy followed closely by Caesarean section. Men have surgery about half as often. The main operations: hernia and appendectomy.

Crime

In the mid-1980s, crime had actually started a slight downturn, in part because the economy was improving. Also, the number of teenagers—who commit a disproportionate number of crimes—was actually dropping, thanks to the aging of the baby boom. Yet a crime still occurred in the USA an average of every three seconds.

And these crimes occurred at these intervals. . .

Murder	every 27 minutes
Forcible rape	every 7 minutes
Robbery	every 63 seconds
Assault	every 49 seconds
Motor vehicle theft	every 31 seconds
Burglary	every 10 seconds
Larceny	every 5 seconds

Now Playing in a Living Room Near You

VCRs, almost unheard of in the '70s, have soared in the mid-'80s. There were about 805,000 in homes in 1980; there are about 12 million now. In fact, more than 31 percent of all households have VCRs.

The sales of compact disc players are also soaring. Appearing in 1983, they are now found in 850,000 homes, almost 2 percent of households.

On the Road Again (and Again and Again)

As we'll see a little later, there is no possession we are so madly in love with as our cars.

There are 112 million cars on the roads. The average age of a car on the highway is now 7.6 years. This is the highest age in more than 30 years.

The USA will have two cars for every three people by the year 2005 as car production races ahead of population growth. Right now there's about one car for every two people.

The number of licensed drivers in the USA has increased 24 percent over the last 10 years—with the sharpest rise among drivers over age 69. The number of drivers in that group has increased by just about its own age—68 percent. The number of drivers 19 and younger has actually dropped slightly since 1974.

Car accidents claimed the lives of 45,800 people in 1985. That's down from 1970 when 54,000 lost their lives and in 1980 when there were 53,000 deaths. Maybe that seat belt statistic we tossed out a few pages back isn't so insignificant after all: Many experts attribute the drop in traffic fatalities to an increase in seat belt use, as well as the 55-mile-per-hour speed limit.

In fact, watch for a new phenomenon of the '80s—the Mandatory Seat Belt Law—to spread in the '90s.

Tube Watching

Although some studies show the television is on about seven hours per day in the average home, it's actually watched only about half that amount of time. In many respects, TV in the '80s has become the background music of life. What does TV do best? You've told us that special sporting events are a clear-cut winner. What does it do worst? Provide regular entertainment shows.

Take a Letter

- The average person receives 556 pieces of mail per year.
- Fewer and fewer of these pieces of mail were written by a

stenographer, and the number will continue to decline. The 239,000 stenographers in the USA will drop by about 40 percent, to 143,000, by 1995, according to the government.

■ Thanks to computers and other office automation, the number of typists will increase by only 1 percent. Overall, though, clerical workers will remain the USA's largest occupational group. There are over 20 million of them.

Take a Message

It may not seem like it sometimes, but the USA doesn't have the highest number of telephones per capita in the world. That distinction belongs to Sweden. In fact, the USA is only third.

Sweden has 86 phones for every 100 people, at least according to a study called The World's Telephones. Switzerland is second with 77 followed by the USA with 70 for each 100 people. The average for industrialized nations: 18.

Passing the Bar

There was one lawyer for every 418 people in the USA in 1980. By 1990, that is expected to increase to one lawyer for every 310 people. In 1970 only 2.8 percent of all lawyers were women. Today women make up 14 percent of all practicing lawyers and 20 percent of all new lawyers entering the profession. Oh, yes, one in 25 residents of Washington, D.C., is a lawyer, the highest concentration of any community in the USA.

Charge It

Nearly 64 percent of us have at least one credit card. The most popular:

	Percent holding card
Retail store	57%
Bank card	42
Gas or oil	28
Travel/entertainment	10

I Do

Over 2.5 million marriages were performed in 1985. And that means big dollars: The average wedding cost $2,480. Now add $920 for the honeymoon, $400 for rings, and $4,240 for home furnishings purchased by the average couple.

What kind of schooling we have really does help determine whom we marry; 55 percent of all adults marry someone with the same educational background. In one out of four marriages the husband has more education than the wife. In one out of five marriages—19 percent—the wife has more education than the husband.

Never on a Sunday

An average of 9,970 babies are born each day in the USA, but, for an interesting reason, there are many fewer babies born on weekends. No, it has nothing to do with genetics. Doctors like to schedule Caesarean or induced labor during the week, according to the federal government. After all, who wants to work on Sunday?

The favorite day to have a baby: Tuesday. Least popular: Sunday.

What Computer Revolution?

Fewer of us purchased computers in 1985, 4.5 million compared with more than 5 million in 1984.

The computer revolution may be sputtering for adults, but schools are using them more and more. Eighty-five percent of the nation's public schools use computers in classrooms compared with 68 percent in 1983 and 18 percent in 1980.

Smart computer companies are helping to develop a future market by giving many of these away free to some schools. Don't get the idea, however, that there's a computer for every student: There are 63 students per computer.

Computers may be set for some kind of a rebound, however. Graduating college seniors tell us that computers are the second most important thing they want to buy, following only cars.

See Hawaii and Live

Residents of Hawaii have the longest life spans: 77.02 years, according to the federal government. Rest of the top five:

Minnesota	76.15 years
Iowa	75.81
Utah	75.76
North Dakota	75.71

The USA's average is 73.88.

Life and Leisure

We spend over $157 billion for recreation, a 50 percent increase over 1980, making leisure one of the nation's fastest-growing industries.

Where does all this money go? More than a quarter out of every dollar goes to buy sports equipment; 22 cents for radios, TV, records, musical instruments, and other such toys; 15 cents to attend sporting events, race tracks, and amusement parks; and 12 cents for such things as books, magazines, and newspapers.

Fifty-four percent of us say we exercise vigorously at least once a week; 39 percent say at least several times a week.

Church Attendance

Almost half of all adults, 44 percent, say they attend church every week; 16 percent, a few times a month; 20 percent, occasionally; 11 percent, rarely; and 9 percent, never.

Home Sweet Home

We bought 3.2 million existing homes in 1985. The average price was $75,200.

We bought 1.76 million new homes. The average price was $83,700.

Have a Bite

Although more and more adults are eating out each night, particularly when both the husband and wife work, 88 percent of all dinners are cooked at home.

Favorite dishes:	
Chicken	15%
Steak	11
Hamburgers	8
Beef roast	6
Pork chops	5

Almost three-quarters, 73 percent, actually cook dinner fresh; 18 percent go for something frozen; 4 percent, canned; 4 percent, boxed.

About 10 percent have an appetizer. The most popular is salad, served in one in four households.

On the other hand, 42 percent have dessert.

Favorite desserts	
Ice cream	21%
Cake	19
Pie	19
Fruit	17

We drink an average of 1.54 cups of coffee per person per day in the USA, down slightly from 1980. More than half, 55 percent of us, drink coffee; but that's down from 75 percent in the early '60s. The biggest drop: those between 20 and 29, which may be why you saw those coffee ads in the '80s trying to attract younger drinkers, featuring famous faces from Kurt Vonnegut to David Bowie.

And After You've Eaten . . .

About 112 million adults started a diet last year, 65 percent of the nation's adult population. Ten percent of them tried to diet at least five times. One in 10 stayed on the diet less than a week.

Overall, 60 percent of all women feel they need to lose weight, 45 percent of the men.

How much weight should they lose? Here's what they said:

Less than 10 pounds	39%
10 to 20 pounds	30

| 20 to 30 pounds | 15 |
| Over 30 pounds | 16 |

Seventy-six percent of all women and 69 percent of all men feel they need to get more exercise.

The Better to See You

Six out of 10 adults wear glasses and almost one in 10 wears contact lenses. Of those who wear glasses, more than half must wear them all the time.

The Biggest

For reasons we won't begin to speculate on, one of the most requested pieces of information by callers to USA TODAY is: What are the 10 largest metropolitan areas in the nation? Well, we'll save you a call. Here they are:

Metropolitan area	Population	Change since 1980	Personal income
1. New York metropolitan area	17,807,000	+ .4	$14,505
2. Los Angeles metro area	12,373,000	+ 1.7	13,379
3. Chicago metro area	8,035,000	+ .3	13,249
4. Philadelphia metro area	5,755,000	+ .3	12,728
5. San Francisco/Oakland	5,685,000	+ 1.3	15,500
6. Detroit-Ann Arbor	4,577,000	− .9	12,586
7. Boston	3,695,000	+ .2	14,297
8. Houston	3,566,000	+ 3.3	13,482
9. Washington, D.C.	3,429,000	+ 1.3	16,173
10. Dallas-Ft. Worth	3,348,000	+ 3.1	13,846

And Now the Fact You've All Been Waiting for

According to R.H. Bruskin Associates, a marketing research firm in New Jersey, 19 percent of all men and 6 percent of all women sleep in the nude.

Young couples were least likely to wear pajamas, especially people aged 25 to 34 who earn $20,000 and up (now, wouldn't you think those would be the people who could best afford them?).

Most popular bedtime wear for women:	
Nighties and nightgowns	63%
Pajamas	19
Underwear	4
Nightshirts	3
Long johns	1
For men:	
Pajamas	37%
Underwear	33
Long johns	2

Well, that's how we stack up. Those are the raw numbers of a nation's life, the stuff of the USA—one country's vital statistics, by age, race, height, weight, home, marital status, and coffee-drinking ability. Now join us for a tour of that diverse nation as we explore what all those people out there think about life in the USA today and tomorrow.

CHAPTER TWO

'80s Life

The 1980s. You know all about them, the age of Ronald Reagan, AIDS, terrorism, the budget deficit, and videocassette recorders.

We all know what's been going on, right? Computers run our lives. Baby boomers shape the USA. Yuppies, the vanguard of this largest, best-educated generation, set our priorities. Our traditional family values are lost in a maze of new lifestyles. That's what we've been seeing happen in the '80s, right?

Wrong!

That's not what's happening at all.

So far, we've done pretty well with understanding much of this century. Certainly it's something of a generalization, but the '50s in many ways really were Happy Days, Ike, and a comfortable isolation. The '60s really did revolve around the Beatles and Woodstock, youthful rebellion, and the reality of Vietnam. The '70s were the Me Generation. Watergate made us cynical and inflation made us cranky.

But what about the '80s?

This is the most studied and analyzed period in history. Yet it has refused to be categorized with the snappy, easy buzzwords we see so often on TV and in newspapers and magazines. This really isn't the generation of Yuppies and the new man, of disillusioned youth and the superwoman. Interviews with literally tens of thousands of people over the last three years in a variety of surveys conducted for USA TODAY show that the '80s are just too complicated for this.

It's no wonder people are confused about what to believe. The '80s are the least understood decade, one we see filtered through a barrage of myths and half-truths.

What are the myths and what are the truths?

Myth: Young, urban professionals (Yuppies) swept across the USA like a wave; on their flag is emblazoned the phrase, "You can have it all"—success, fun, possessions, status.

Truth: Try to find these Yuppies and you'll find an astonishing fact. There aren't many of them out there. Less than 4 percent of all baby boomers make $35,000 or more. Many more make less than $10,000. And, more important, many of them really aren't very happy.

Myth: The family is changed forever. We don't want kids; we don't want to be tied down as our parents were.

Truth: We're surprisingly happy and satisfied with our family lives. We enjoy being with our relatives, we make sacrifices for them, and if we get divorced, most of us want to get married again.

It is true that we are having children later and getting divorced more. But basic family values remain intact. While women are in fact delaying childbirth more often, it's usually to get their careers in order before childbirth. The desire to have a family remains just as strong through the career years.

Myth: Life in the '80s belongs to the young. Old age means sitting in the sun in God's Waiting Room by the Sea in Florida or California or Arizona.

Truth: Older adults are among the happiest, most active of any age group. More and more of them will be staying on the job longer or returning to work; and in many cases, it doesn't have anything to do with needing the cash. In fact, they actually have more money to spend than their children.

Myth: For the first time in history, young children are facing futures which are not as bright as those of their parents. They're being forced to reduce their goals and expectations in life because of the soaring number of people competing for the very few jobs at the top.

Truth: This may be the most insidious myth of all. It's long been the great dream of our citizens to provide for their children a better life than they had, to give their children the things they never enjoyed. And it's long been the great belief of the children that such a dream could come true.

Now, for the first time, we've been hearing that we have to give up that dream. And it's simply not true. There is evidence of a new spirit of independence and entrepreneurism in the land. We are finding new and exciting ways to create opportunities for ourselves, and for our children.

Here's another truth about the '80s: All those myths are driving us a little crazy.

If the '80s are anything, they are *The Age Of The Image.* Our lives have actually become more complicated by the struggle to keep up with the expectations that have been built around us. The beer ad says, "You can have it all," and so we all try.

One psychologist, responding to a USA TODAY survey, put it this way: "Everyone is more stressed, and dissatisfied with the difference between expectations and reality. Commercials have sold them a bill of goods that happiness is bliss. 'Ordinary' lives aren't OK any more, so they're depressed."

On the other hand, here's another truth about the '80s. We're not taking them lying down. From the confusion of trying to keep up with the images around us is emerging a new priority: the desire to take control of our own lives.

We have a tremendous fear of being ordinary, of living and dying unnoticed, with someone else setting the agenda of our life's work. More and more the '80s will be an era in which we will be trying to gain and keep personal authority over the events that shape our lives.

Here's our prediction: The You-Can-Have-It-All commercials will be replaced with a new set of come-ons. Your Life Belongs to You. The drink for people who make their own decisions. The watch for people who set their own agenda.

The Baby Bust

The baby boom may turn out to be the biggest bust in USA history, at least to the thousands of companies, firms, and business people who expected to make a killing on selling to this generation—the biggest, best-educated generation ever, and the generation that has probably been the subject of more analysis than any other.

Baby boomers were forecast to take the nation by storm. They were featured in every major magazine from *Newsweek* to *People*. They got their own edition of Trivial Pursuit. They even anointed their own presidential candidate in Gary Hart—and faster than you could say "The Big Chill," Madison Avenue came running.

Rarely has so much been written about so few over so little. And rarely have so many been confused over so much.

American Demographics, the bible of people-watchers, called 1984 The Year of the Baby Boom. Less than a year later, it turned around to proclaim that the baby boom generation "has become famous simply for being famous."

Once forecast as the wave that would change the USA forever, the baby boom—78 million people born between 1946 and 1964, a full third of the USA's population—isn't the single-minded group we originally thought.

And, to Madison Avenue's chagrin, they don't buy the way they're supposed to buy.

Baby boomers defy the stereotype that has grown around them. In a recent Roper Poll people were asked to describe Yuppies. The answer: people in their 20s and 30s, extremely well-educated, self-absorbed and career-oriented; high-salaried people who use the latest products.

Well, they are, on average, more educated, and by definition they're in their 20s and 30s—but that's about as far as it goes.

More than a third of baby boomers make less than $10,000 a year. More than half make less than $20,000. And although this is the best-educated generation in history, more than half never went to college at all. And 13 percent didn't graduate from high school.

How happy are they? We recently asked people to describe their lives. Baby boomers were most likely to say their lives are getting harder. Then we asked people if they were happy. Who came out at the bottom? People aged 25 to 34.

That's right, baby boomers.

In fact, it went that way on a series of related questions.

Who were most likely to say they'd been laid off in the last year? Baby boomers. Least satisfied with their job? Most likely to be divorced or separated? Most likely to have marital problems? Baby boomers.

Who had the least job security? The elderly—but baby boomers came in a close second.

Baby boomers were most likely to say they weren't having enough fun in life, didn't have enough time to do the things they wanted to do, and didn't have enough good friends.

Yet, in the face of all this, that old-fashioned American optimism—the stuff we've been hearing has died off—remains. Despite all these setbacks, baby boomers more than any other group in the USA say their prospects for the future are very good.

We asked: Do the following statements describe you? Here are some specific results:

	Baby boomers	All adults
I'm very satisfied with my job	45%	51%
I'm very satisfied with my financial security	24	27
I'm divorced or separated	30	23
I have serious marriage problems	6	4
I find myself without enough good friends	21	18
I don't have enough fun in life	19	17
I don't have enough time to do the things I'd like to do	69	59
I don't have enough entertainment, cultural activities and recreation	36	29
I'm very happy with the quality of my friendships	63	68
My financial prospects for the future are very good	40	34

Keys To Happiness

Take this simple test yourself. Circle the letter before each event that has happened to you in the last three months:

Did you:
A. Get married
B. Get a raise
C. Get a new job or promotion
D. Move to a better place to live
E. Not have enough time to do the things you want
F. Have a death in your family
G. Work at a job you didn't enjoy
H. Get divorced
I. Get robbed, assaulted or threatened by crime

| J. Feel lonely much of the time |
| K. Have a serious problem with your marriage |

Using sophisticated computer techniques, we studied thousands of adults to try to figure out what makes them happy and sad. We found that common events, like the ones listed above, can affect our lives in some unusual and unexpected ways.

For example, having a serious problem in a marriage (Question K) actually causes more unhappiness than getting divorced.

Experts say there's a reason for that: Divorce is the resolution of a problem, even if it's not a desirable resolution. If you have serious problems with your marriage and stay together, the agony continues.

The traditional values of home, work, and community are very much alive. More than any other events, the things that make us most happy with our lives in the 1980s are: family life, recognition in our jobs, and moving to a better place to live.

This may be part of that Image Age syndrome. These things show the world that we are successful and show us that the world approves. But this also runs contrary to the myth that the '80s are a time when such traditional values are going the way of Free Love and Disco.

The things that make us most unhappy in the '80s: not having any fun, feeling lonely, and having a problem with our marriage. Lonely people believe, "There must be something wrong with me."

OK, let's see how you scored on our Happiness Index. Look back at the events you circled above—and give yourself points (or take points away) based on this score sheet.

A. Got married	+7
B. Got a raise	+5
C. Got a new job or promotion	+1
D. Moved to a better place to live	+1
E. Didn't have enough time to do the things you want	-3
F. Had a death in your family	-4
G. Worked at a job you didn't enjoy	-12

H. Got divorced	-16
I. Were robbed, assaulted, or threatened by crime	-19
J. Felt lonely much of the time	-22
K. Had serious problem with your marriage	-22

The average score for adults of all ages was zero. If you wound up with a plus number you're probably happier than the average '80s adult. As you might guess by now, baby boomers wound up at the bottom. Happiest group in the USA, by far: people aged 55 to 64. Men and women wound up exactly even.

Real Value

In many ways, people in the '80s are no different from their parents or grandparents. Take the '50s, for example. Pick out a key image: Ike, Ozzie and Harriet, cheerful little bomb shelters, nothing more risque than Elvis' pelvis.

Clearly a lot has changed—but not in the ways that are most important to us.

We've been talking about those things that make us happy, but when we change that question a little, and ask people, "What makes you most satisfied in your life?" we get different sorts of answers.

It is in this area, we think, that people's deeper values come to the fore. Having fun may make us happy, but family life and stability at home give us a deeper satisfaction and fulfillment.

From survey to survey, when we ask people what makes them most satisfied with their lives, the results remain remarkably consistent. The top priorities almost always deal with our homes and families.

Here's what people tell us are the parts of their lives they are very satisfied with:

Part of life	
Our children	82%
Relationship with spouse	81
Family	79
Friendships	74

Health	64
Where we live	58
Physical condition	54
How we practice our religion	53
Social life	52
How we look	45

Again, men and women come out about even—but there are some interesting differences. Only about a third of the women say they're happy with the way they look; more than half the men like their own looks. Males are also more likely to be satisfied with their physical condition and their health. Women are more likely to be happy with the friendships they've formed.

People in their 30s are less satisfied than anyone else with their social lives. Although society has an image of these people as being in the prime of their lives, they tell us that the pressure of raising children and building careers are overwhelming.

Overall, when we ask people their top personal goals, the same things come to the fore: health and family life. Here are the percentages of people who called the following among the top priorities in their lives:

Get more exercise	66%
Improve family life	64
Spend more time with family	63
Lose weight	53
Eat a more balanced diet	52
Work harder at job	48
Get a medical checkup	47
Stop smoking	18
Cut down on drinking	12

And the same contrasts between men and women are evident here. By a wide margin (61-45) women are more concerned about losing weight than men are. They also make getting exercise a higher goal. Men are twice as likely as women to want to cut down on drinking and are more likely to want to get a medical checkup and work harder at their job.

Controlling Our Lives

As we went through the 100-plus surveys on which this book is based, we kept noticing an interesting thing: The desire people have for getting control over their own lives kept showing up in lots of different ways. It caught our interest, and we started asking people about it directly.

Since then, we've surveyed more than 15,000 people on the subject. (For comparison, the average pollster talks to about 1,000 to predict who'll win the presidency.) Here's what we learned: "The desire for control" is beginning to emerge as one of the primary forces that will shape the way we work, think, act, and live in the 1990s.

Control of our lives is what we want. It's what we feel will make us happy. The desire for that control will be a main motivator.

In more than 5,000 interviews, we asked people how much control they felt they have in their lives, and also asked how happy they are.

The people who felt they were gaining control were much more likely than others to say they are "very happy." In fact, people who felt they were losing control were about half as likely to call themselves "very happy."

Here's the connection we found between people saying they're very happy and how those people rated the control they have gained (or lost) over their lives in the past year:

How happy are you?	I'm more in control	I'm less in control
Very happy	60%	37%
Fairly happy	37	48
Not happy	2	15

Moving Toward the '90s

So what are we doing to gain control of our lives?

The number of self-employed people in the USA increased 24 percent between 1974 and 1984, a growth rate much higher than the growth in the total work force.

In the '80s, the number of people who work for themselves grew at a rate four times faster than the number of people who work for a daily wage. And the idea that men are the entrepreneurs in our society is yet another myth: Women are going into business for themselves at a much higher rate than men.

The tremendous surge of entrepreneurial spirit in the USA will continue to be one of the great stories of the 1980s and '90s. It's becoming a new frontier for us.

Our research shows that people see starting their own business as a way not just to make money but to make a stand, to gain not only financial independence but to find the control over their own destiny that they so clearly crave.

A survey of the Inc. 500—the 500 fastest-growing privately held firms in the USA—shows that 89 percent of the firms' founders say they started their business for reasons relating to personal independence. The No. 1 reason: "I wanted to control my own life." We'll hear more from these people later on and find why smart companies are learning to capitalize on this spirit by setting up centers within corporations, which executives can run almost like their own companies.

Little Hassles, Big Fears

Behind the entrepreneurism and optimism, of course, lie some dark spots—some big, some tiny—but all telling us something about life in the '80s.

Let's start off with the tiny ones.

It's fitting that in a recent poll of what hassles us in the '80s, conducted by Louis Harris Associates and sponsored by Nuprin, "too many things to do" ranks near the top with the more traditional hassles and fears. Here's what hassles us in the '80s:

Rising prices	47%
Too many things to do	41
Money for emergencies	35
Trouble relaxing	31
Family illness	27
General concerns about health	24
Trouble making decisions	23
Not enough money for basics	22
Being lonely	18

Noise	18
Problems with children	18
Problems with aging parents	18

Those are the day-to-day hassles that drive us crazy. Our deeper fears are much more serious.

People in the USA have many worries about the future, and perhaps teenagers are the most worried among us.

Teens worry, most of all, about the threat of war; 48 percent called it their top fear. The economy was a distant second at 11 percent.

Among teens, 85 percent say the United States will be involved in an international conflict as peacemakers, much as we were in Lebanon. Just under half of the USA's teenagers say we will fight in a Vietnam-style war. And here's the most disturbing fact of all: 26 percent of our teenagers, fully one in four, say the United States will be involved in a global nuclear war sometime in the next decade.

High-Tech

Here's how we would have remade *The Graduate* back in 1982: Let's put Richard Gere in Dustin Hoffman's role. He's just graduated college; we move the poolside party to a hot tub. And the secret to success, whispered in his ear, is no longer *plastics*.

It's *computers*.

Time magazine made the PC into a cover boy by naming it the magazine's "Machine of the Year"—taking the place of the traditional Man of the Year.

The Man of the Year turned out to be a baby. Record sales have turned into record slumps. Computer companies, software firms, even techie magazines went out of business. Where have you gone, Popular Computing?

It's important to make it clear here that the computer is a revolutionary device. There is no question that we've adopted a high-tech lifestyle in the '80s, one we'll never give up.

The computer industry is primed and bursting with potential. Consumers are waiting to embrace the machines. But the key word here is "primed." The potential is there but the computer industry has misunderstood the people of the '80s, and that's keeping it from achieving that potential.

When computer sales were soaring a few years ago, the people who were doing the buying were those who fell in love with the technology. These are the same people who, as children, took apart watches to see what makes them work. But there are only so many of them, and they've already bought their machines.

Again Madison Avenue ran smack into the Myth—the belief that we really are the people in the beer ads, people who want to have it all whether they need it all or not. The computer boom never counted on all those people out there who didn't feel they needed a computer—people who felt they could balance their checkbook just fine the old-fashioned way, thank you.

To attract new customers, computer manufacturers are going to have to provide something new—a reason to buy.

You've probably seen the microwave oven ads on television. The ones where a smiling but harried woman executive comes home, throws her dinner into the microwave, slips off her shoes and relaxes. Three minutes later dinner is done, even the potatoes; her life is magically back in order.

That's what the computer industry needs—a three-minute potato.

Because that's where the problem lies—lots of hungry people, no three-minute potato. Actually, there's plenty of interest out there in owning a computer. People would really love to buy one. It's just that when they come down to concrete reasons for needing one, they come up empty.

Consider this:

- 53 percent of all adults show some background or interest in computers. They either own one, have used one for work, or have shopped for one.
- Almost 23 million adults use a computer at work but don't have one at home, representing a huge, potential market of already knowledgeable consumers. And far from impersonalizing the work environment as some critics claimed it would, 91 percent of people who use a computer at work say it has improved their work conditions.
- People in the USA are pro-computer and think their neighbors are too. We asked the nation's adults to estimate what

percentage of USA homes will have computers in the next five years. The average answer: more than half, 53 percent.

■ 76 percent of all adults say it's important for people to learn to use a computer.

So why don't more people buy? Here's why:

Simply no reason to buy	72%
Too expensive	43
Afraid current models will be outdated	24
Just waiting for prices to come down	23
Too difficult to learn	15
Computers are just a fad	14

More than any other reason, people look at computers and just don't see any three-minute potato in it for them. Very few feel that computers are just this year's high-priced toy.

Most people don't care about expandability or adaptability or any of the other terms inflicted on us during TV commercials. People who are considering buying their first computer don't make their decision based on how fast a computer can run. They want something to help them get through the day. And a $2,500 machine to store recipes and keep track of appointments is an easy purchase to delay.

The challenge now is for computer manufacturers and software makers to come up with compelling reasons for people to buy their products. They have to sell life-value, not hardware.

To find out what people would buy a computer for, we asked average people to "blue sky," to tell us what they would want to use a computer for, whether the technology currently exists or not.

Here's what we found out:

Educational material for a child	14%
Doing banking or paying bills	13
Managing finances and budgeting	13
Doing word processing	13
Educational material for yourself	13
Taking classes or seminars at home	11
Getting medical information on illness or drugs	11

Doing tax returns	10
Reading lists of available jobs	9
Viewing library books or other sources of information	9
Sending letters and messages to friends	8
Buying theater or sports tickets and selecting seats	8
Making travel reservations and renting cars, etc.	8
Study for college entrance exams and other tests	8
Finding best routes for trips	7
Getting late business, financial news	7
To vote	6
Reading real estate listings	5
Reading restaurant menus and making reservations	3

Some of those can be done on a computer right now, but it's a real chore. People have gone to France without learning French, and they want to help their kids with their homework without learning another language too.

Notice that a lot of those "blue sky" items are things people do every day. That's what people want their computer to be, something that fits into their everyday life.

Here's one of the most encouraging facts we've found about the computer industry's future: We asked teens what kind of work they planned to do when they left school. We asked it open-ended—offering no choices. The No. 1 answer that came back was computer science.

The computer, it should be noted here, has some startling effects on people's lives once they let it into their homes. Later, when we begin discussing family life in the '80s, we'll be talking about the place TV occupies in the home. For better or for worse, watching television is the No. 1 activity that families do as a group. Nothing else comes close.

Well, for better or for worse, TV is the No. 1 thing we give up when we get a computer at home. Nothing else comes close.

Here's what the computer takes time away from:

Watching TV	69%
Going to movies	24
Reading	24
Entertainment	24

Participation in sports	17
Family activities (besides TV)	14

Teenage boys are the most prolific users of computers in the home and nobody seems to know just why. This slips into a much larger question about the differences between teenage boys and teenage girls—why boys seem to become better at math around the age of 14, for example—a discussion certainly beyond the scope of this book.

There is a parallel, however. Our surveys show that boys and girls seem to start out with the same degree of interest in computers. Even at age 13 there's very little difference. But beginning about age 14, boys use computers more than twice as often.

Have you ever noticed that when you walk past a video game parlor (which, by the way, is another of those early '80s phenomena that have cooled down), its inhabitants are almost exclusively male? This could be one way that boys learn an early comfortable feeling about computer skills that girls are left out of. It could be a way that boys are taught, encouraged, or allowed to socialize—which for one reason or another girls are kept away from.

What's clear is that boys are much more heavily involved in computers than girls are, starting from their early teens.

And, as you'd expect, teens use the computer for reasons different from those of their parents. Here's how we use computers at home:

Use	Total	Adults	Children
Games	48%	28%	66%
Educational programs	40	33	47
Word processing	33	42	25
Storing information	29	38	20
Financial management	19	31	6
Accounting	14	23	4

For adults, computers represent a new opportunity (or problem, depending on how you look at it): a new way to bring work home.

Computers are having a dramatic impact in our lives by enabling us to blur the traditional boundary between the home and the job. A USA TODAY poll shows that fully 44 percent of those with a home computer use it to bring their office-work home.

At the beginning of this decade this number would have been too small to count.

It adds another day to our workweek—and it's about the same for men and women (for men, this adds just over eight hours to the workweek; for women, about seven hours and 45 minutes).

One trend to watch: Companies will increasingly encourage employees to have home computers that are compatible with their computers at work, either by helping with the purchase or by simply giving the computer to the employee free of charge.

One last note on the high-tech age. Despite the problems the computer industry has to overcome, it has one big thing going for it. People have proven that they love high-tech gadgets and adapt to them quickly. This list shows people's favorite personal possession. And fancy electronics, things not widely available a decade ago, grabbed six of the top eight spots:

A second TV set	68%
A second car	58
Microwave oven	52
Videocassette recorder	38
Video camera	22
Home computer	17
Big-screen TV	14
Telephone answering machine	12
Second home	11
Swimming pool	10
Spa or Jacuzzi	6
Car telephone	2

And when we asked them, then, what they'd most like to buy—high-tech products rated one, two, three.

Videocassette recorder	13%
Microwave oven	10
Home computer	11
Second car	9
Swimming pool	5

The Disease of the '80s

Of all the headlines of the '80s, none strikes fear into our hearts more than the Acquired Immune Deficiency Syndrome—AIDS. In just a few short months it became an acronym for fear, pain, panic, and death.

The hysteria has been more rampant than the disease itself. The public got the idea, incorrectly, that you could catch AIDS from giving blood—and blood banks suffered severe shortages. Mothers kept their children out of school when they learned one of the students had the disease.

How worried are we about AIDS?

Seventy-six percent say AIDS will become a serious epidemic.

Sixty-one percent say they are more worried about AIDS than they were a year ago. And 37 percent say AIDS is the most serious health problem facing the nation today.

And when we asked people to name serious health threats facing the nation, AIDS trailed only cancer and heart disease.

Cancer	92%
Heart disease	88
AIDS	64
Diabetes	51
Multiple sclerosis	43
Polio	12

Because of the fear, worry, and uncertainty surrounding the disease there's a great deal of confusion over how it spreads. But once again, the myth is as good as a mile. Here are four ways you *can't* get AIDS, according to all the research to date, and how many people think you can:

- 43 percent say you can get AIDS from kissing.
- 32 percent say you can get AIDS from using a public toilet seat.
- 14 percent say you can get AIDS just from being in the same room as an AIDS victim.
- 12 percent say you can get AIDS just from shaking hands.

Think about it: More than one out of 10 people in this country believe you can get AIDS from shaking hands. No wonder 64 percent of the adults in the USA—64 percent!—say that the government should legally restrict the movement of AIDS victims.

People also say they're taking definite actions to avoid AIDS, actions that may very well change our lifestyles for the rest of the decade and beyond:

- 37 percent say they are avoiding homosexuals
- 17 percent won't donate blood
- 55 percent say people should avoid casual sex

And a third of all adults say AIDS victims have no one to blame but themselves for catching the disease.

The Rebirth of Education

The '80s have also seen a tremendous renaissance of interest in how well we educate our children. A series of reports condemning the education system raised an outcry unmatched since the 1950s when the United States found itself suddenly behind in the space race.

The National Commission on Excellence in Education, a key blue-ribbon panel, called us "a nation at risk." In its report, it warned: "The educational foundations of our society are presently being eroded by a rising tide of mediocrity. We have, in effect, been committing an act of unthinking, unilateral educational disarmament."

The report set off a series of strong reactions. Everyone from President Reagan to the local school board member seemed to be putting at the top of their agenda some idea for fixing the schools.

The interest hasn't been all hot air; a survey of parents shows they really feel their children's schools are improving.

When we asked parents a few years back how they rated the schools in their community, only 34 percent said they were improving. When we repeated the survey recently, that number jumped dramatically. Fully half of the parents said their schools are getting better.

A note of caution—this doesn't necessarily mean the schools really *did* get better. Sometimes, the increased attention to a problem makes people feel better. But it's clear that parents were watching the schools closely, and increased parental attention is often cited by educators as a top way to improve community schools.

And parents agree. We asked them what's needed to improve their schools, and here are their answers:

More involvement by parents	92%
Improved textbooks	72
Better teacher education	71
Higher teacher salaries	66
Longer school days	26
Longer school years	19

Aside from the general need for improvement in schools, two issues stood out in the area of education in the 1980s—the argument over school prayer and a need to return to basics. Among all adults, 76 percent said prayer should be allowed. And parents in our survey came out strongly for readin', writin', and 'rithmatic (though not exactly in that order):

What should schools be teaching more?	
Reading	90%
Arithmetic	82
Drug abuse education	82
Writing	81
Grammar	81
Computer education	60
Sex education	59
Driver education	47

Crime and Safety

When Bernhard Goetz shot four black youths in a New York subway, he also hit another target: our fear of crime and frustration with our courts and laws.

Seventy-seven percent of the USA's adults were supportive of Goetz—many saying it's about time people started defending themselves. And that includes 57 percent of the blacks.

These results indicate just how deeply crime and the fear of crime affect our lives.

Earlier we talked about what makes us most happy, and what makes us most satisfied. In almost every study we've done asking people to rank the USA's top priority, crime ranked either first or second. The only thing that concerned people more was unemployment; nothing else even came close.

In our most recent survey, here's what concerned Americans the most:

Unemployment	44%
Crime	42
Excessive government spending	35
The threat of war	31
Nuclear weapons	31
Inflation	29
Poor political leadership	24
Social injustice	22
Inadequate defense	14
Energy crisis	12

It was startling in some ways to have a man shoot four youths in a subway and find himself on top of a wave of public support; but 82 percent say the public approval of Goetz is a direct result of frustration with law and order in the USA.

Government statistics show that the average time served in prison per crime has fallen to its lowest point ever. Convicted murderers served an average of less than six years in prison, and most of us just don't like it.

Here's the breakdown, according to the U.S. government, of the average prison terms in the USA:

Crime	Months served
Murder	69
Rape	36
Manslaughter	28
Robbery	25
Burglary	14

This concerns us as a nation: 78 percent said the laws and courts are more concerned with the rights of the criminal than with the rights of the victim—and this next chart shows that many of us have reason to identify with the victim:

Have you or any member of your immediate family been a victim of:	
Burglary	37%
Robbery	32
Being threatened	30
Car theft	21
Assault	15
Murder	4
Rape	3

Here's how we felt about that: 77 percent say police simply can't ensure safety in large cities; 61 percent say people have a right to protect themselves with guns; and 71 percent say they are willing to spend more money on police and jails.

The Turning Point

So what are the '80s? They are a turning point. We are struggling with the images and ideas around us—images that move toward us at a faster and faster pace while we struggle to gain control of our lives.

The entrepreneurism of the '80s is creating new jobs, fueling the economy, and debunking the notion that the best years are behind us. And the inherent optimism which shows up in all of our surveys will help us move ahead.

In fact, we're pretty confident about the future, about what it holds in store for us financially and emotionally, individually and as a nation. By a two-to-one margin, the USA's adults feel their lives will improve as we move toward the 21st century. The new, emerging focus of the '80s—that desire to take control of our own lives—will be the shaping tool of the '90s.

As we move through this book, we'll look at various segments of society—men, women, teenagers, the elderly, business people, married people, divorced people. All of them are participants in the Image Age, and as we will see, all are trying in their own way to separate the image from the reality.

CHAPTER THREE

Women

The woman of the '80s has begun to achieve what the woman of the '60s began to demand—the right, like any man sitting next to her in the office, to say "I want to have it all." Again, it's like the woman we see in the commercial: the one who brings home the bacon and cooks it, too, and cleans the pan; tucks the baby into bed and manages to look incredibly sexy the whole time.

More than government, more than the economy, more even than the struggle for racial equality in the United States, the emerging woman is changing the way we work, the way we live, even the way we think.

As we noted in the first chapter, more than half of all women now work.

Women also account for a growing number of purchases. They buy four out of 10 new cars and help decide on the purchase of another 40 percent.

The New York Stock Exchange reports that 57 percent of all new investors are women. Their average age: 34. Average income: $35,000 a year.

And, perhaps more important, women feel better about being themselves; better about being women. When we asked recently if it was better to be a man in today's society, only 24 percent of the women agreed. While still one in four, that's

significantly fewer than in previous generations; and most of
the women who feel that way now are more than 35 years old.

Men are feeling better about women too. That's come out
in a lot of ways. Here's a fun one: We recently asked men and
women viewers which TV cop they would prefer as their partner. The winner? Miami Vice's Sonny Crockett? Hill Street's
Frank Furillo? Nope—Mary Beth Lacey from Cagney and
Lacey.

While there's still a long way to go, amazing things began
happening to women in the workplace during the '80s. It was
perhaps fitting that New Year's Eve 1985 saw the dawn of a
new era. On that day, women achieved perhaps their most
stunning victory of the decade.

In what had become a landmark battle, a court had ordered
the state of Washington to give women the same pay as men if
they did work that was just as hard or just as important. On
that fateful afternoon, just hours before heading off to New
Year's Eve parties, officials of the state of Washington agreed
to usher in the new age—and signed a $482 million "compa-
rable worth" agreement with its employees union.

It had been illegal for a long time to pay men and women
differently if they did the same job. But what this settlement,
which is having a ripple effect all across the USA, meant is
this: Jobs long considered "women's work"—typist, teacher,
and nurse are three—are worth the same pay as "men's jobs"
such as electrician or truck driver.

And even though comparable worth has not been accepted
in all states, its impact is being felt in the legislatures and
board rooms across the nation. The fact that a dozen states
and a hundred cities are looking at doing something similar is
perhaps the key symbol of what women are doing in the
'80s—not only are they "making it in a man's world," but
they are proving that the marketplace is just as much a
woman's world. The low-paying "women's ghetto" jobs,
those held primarily by women, are finally beginning to get as
much respect—in the way it counts, in the pocketbook—as
the jobs primarily held by men. There's still a huge gap—
women earn less than 65 cents for every dollar a man earns—
but winning this battle was a terribly important step toward
changing that.

The women who won this battle are the prototypical women of the '80s. They had not just said, "I want what a man wants"; they said, "I want what I want, on my terms."

Well, what kind of dreams are we talking about? The dream of the Woman of the '80s has been an enormous one—a Superwoman, balancing a home and career, family and community—and while the achievements have been stunning, the pitfalls have been more serious than most of us ever imagined.

Our research shows clearly that women don't want to give up their homes and families. A vast majority want kids. They're happiest when they combine home, family, and work.

The very idea that women can have it all—career, marriage, children—is a potent force. It is certainly a natural outgrowth of the women's rights movement that started back at the turn of the century. But it is also an outgrowth of the Image Age: Women buy into the Superwoman image because this is the image of success.

It has become not just a right but an expectation for the modern woman to succeed. People do what's expected of them; they try to live up to the expectations they sense around them.

Here's why that's so tough: As liberated as we may think the '80s are, women still carry the lion's share of the responsibility—and if something doesn't get done, if the kids don't get to school on time or the dishes are still in the sink in the morning, the woman carries the lion's share of the guilt.

Although 54 percent of all women work, they still carry a full load at home. Men and women polled by USA TODAY agree: Women carry the burden of keeping house and raising children—even when they work full time.

We've known for a long time that the workplace rat race can create an awful psychological burden. When you add to this the additional problems an '80s woman faces—trying to make inroads in a workplace that remains sexist and only grudgingly gives the occasional inch; trying to live up to the Image Age expectations of the Superwoman; and trying to maintain the traditional responsibility for home and hearth—it's not surprising to hear what women have told us:

It's all creating a lot of stress.

It's enough to make you crazy.

One family counselor told us that one of the biggest differences in the mental health problems for men and women is that for women it's "The age of the Superwoman—the problems of home and career, as well as sharing financial responsibilities." Another called it "the juggling act—doing it all."

It is this conflict—fighting to be equal in the workplace, while trying to maintain the traditional role of Making the House a Home—that is at the root of the frustration we are hearing from women. Either they're finding frustration in the workplace, or frustration at home, but the attempt to live up to the image of Superwoman is giving the Woman of the '80s a hard day's night.

The Burden from Within

Superwoman is not an easy image to live up to. The demands on women today are great and a lot of those demands come from within. For many, the question is not how to perform their various roles, but rather how to perform them all well. In one study we asked thousands of men and women how well they do various tasks. In every case, women were more likely to rate themselves as very good—and in follow-up interviews, they told us it was very important to them that they perform the tasks well. Feeling they filled these roles well was an important part of their sense of self-worth.

Percentages of people who said they did an excellent job as:

	Men	Women
Husband/wife	39%	53%
Father/mother	47	65
Worker	54	57
Brother/sister	44	54
Son/daughter	38	56

One of the results of placing this greater burden on themselves: Women are less likely than men to rate the quality of their lives as very good. Think about this: Women rate 36 percent lower than men in satisfaction with their sex lives and are 20 percent less satisfied than men with their financial status. Women are also much less likely to say the quality of their life is improving now.

But that doesn't mean men are more optimistic. When we ask about the future, women are just as likely as men to say their lives are going to get better.

That belief in the future, the feeling that "I'm gonna get it all" may be part of living in the Image Age, and it's this high level of self-demand that makes women frustrated.

Doing Double Duty

It's not just the dreaming that sets women apart. Men are also going through the '80s trying to live up to a fantasy of super-success. But the reality that makes it much more difficult for women, the thing that makes the dream drive them crazy, is that they're doing double duty.

No matter how you cut it, women carry the burden at home, even when they work full time.

Sure, men do more around the home than their fathers did. Men and women agree to this in our surveys.

But are they anywhere close to sharing the load 50-50? No way.

Consider this: In this age of liberation and equal opportunity, 94 percent of all women who live with a man say they do more work around the home than their husbands or live-in boyfriends. And the men agree.

Surprisingly, however, only about one in five women—21 percent—wish the men would do more around the house. This is key to understanding the conflict for women of the '80s. As they expand their horizons, they are not at all sure they want to give up the thing that has always given them self-esteem: the ability to take care of the home and family.

For it is the woman, by a wide margin, who feels it's her responsibility to take care of the kids.

Who takes care of dinner? Still the woman, in 71 percent of the USA's households. Men still empty the garbage and mow the lawn—but just as the music of the '80s harkens back to the '50s, so does the division of labor.

Here's who does what around the house:

	Women	Men	Both
Laundry	80%	8%	12%
Cooking	75	9	16

Vacuuming	67	15	18
Cleaning	65	11	24
Dishes	66	14	20
Food shopping	61	11	28
Emptying the garbage	32	57	11
Mowing the lawn	22	76	2

Other Roles, Other Burdens

Women handle a lot more around the home that's not related to cooking dinner and washing dishes. The woman tends to be the person family members confide in.

For example, teens—both boys and girls—say that when they want to talk about a problem, they go to their mothers first. Dad doesn't even come in second. He comes in fourth, behind male friends and female friends.

Women tend to buffer family members, even their macho husbands, against the bumps and bruises of life. And as a result, they tend to experience more stress than men do.

In almost every way, the woman feels that she shoulders the burden more than her spouse does. The areas in which the woman feels she takes on more of the responsibility are wide-ranging.

We named a number of aspects of life and asked: How important is this to you? We then compared the men's and women's answers to get an idea of who feels more responsible for what.

In each of these cases, more women than men said these things are "very important" to them. The breakdown:

Job	29 percent more than men
Financial security	52 percent more than men
Own health	22 percent more than men
Health of those you love	16 percent more than men
Marriage	11 percent more than men
Maintenance of home	15 percent more than men
The community in which you live	44 percent more than men
Quality of environment	36 percent more than men
Friendships	42 percent more than men

This is where the woman of the '80s crashes up against the Superwoman expectation. Here's what happens when women shoulder all that responsibility:

- Women are 43 percent more likely than men to say they feel lonely much of the time.
- Women are 43 percent more likely than men to say they don't have fun much of the time.
- Women are 31 percent more likely than men to say life is getting harder.
- Women are 14 percent less likely to say they have control over their lives.

Women are also more likely to feel stress about how household chores are divided. Questioning whether they're liked, appreciated, and emotionally supported gives them more stress than it gives men. They're more stressed about communicating feelings; they have more anxiety about financial matters.

This stress reaches its peak between ages 26 and 39, when life is at its busiest, when women are forging a career, raising children, building lives.

There is an up side to the sense of immense responsibility that women are faced with in the '80s. The sense of impending achievement (despite all the stress it creates) has brought with it a sense of great independence. Disappearing rapidly, we've found, is the feeling that a woman has to have a man take care of her. In fact, 94 percent of all women consider themselves independent—compared with 85 percent of men.

What we haven't figured out yet, as a society, is just what this means for all of us. For example, look at how much disagreement there is in response to the following statement:

"As women become more independent, things will actually improve for men":

	Total	Male	Female
Strongly agree	17%	15%	19%
Moderately agree	30	30	30
Moderately disagree	25	26	24
Strongly disagree	17	19	16
Not sure	11	10	11

As you can see, just about as many people agree as disagree with the statement; and men aren't that different from women in their responses.

Here's another statement that shows the widespread confusion over the effect of women's independence (and this time, men and women answered almost exactly in the same way): "Relationships between men and women will improve as a result of increasing independence of women":

	Total
Strongly agree	16%
Moderately agree	31
Moderately disagree	26
Strongly disagree	21
Not sure	6

Again, the answers are spread all over the board. In other words, we're not quite sure of the answer at all.

Two factors that seem to play strongly here are age and work. Younger women—those aged 18 to 39—are twice as likely as older women to say relationships get better when women are independent.

That independence grows, no matter what the woman's age, if she is working. Women in households where both spouses work are significantly more likely to call themselves "independent" than are other women. This holds true even if the woman works part time.

Motherhood Doesn't Come Second

It's true that women are marrying and having children later, almost two years later than in the 1950s.

The delay does not appear to be a rejection of marriage, but rather a way to buy time to get a career started. And, while it's true that women are having fewer children, they still rate the role of mother as the most satisfying part of their lives. The role of wife comes second; nothing else even comes close.

Only about 6 percent of the women ever married remain childless, the Census Bureau reports. And 85 percent of the women tell us they want to have children some day, a figure confirmed by similar surveys. This is a matter of degree—in previous generations that figure was even higher—but it shows that while the '80s woman has many new priorities, she's still very likely to pursue the more traditional ones.

Despite the stresses we've talked about, the happiest women in the USA seem to be those who combine work, marriage, and parenthood. Clearly these women rank highest among females in USA TODAY's Life Quality Index, the special study done to rate how life events affect our satisfaction and happiness that we talked about in Chapter 2.

Here are the percentages of women who rate the following roles in their life as the "most satisfying":

Mother	35%
Wife	30
Work	7
Daughter	6
Friend to men	6
Friend to women	5
Sister	3
Not sure	8

We can expect the same values to remain strong in the years ahead. In a recent USA TODAY national study of teenagers, 98 percent said they want to have children; 95 percent of the girls planned to have two or more children.

Some values do change, however. Consider, for example, pregnancy outside of wedlock. In decades past, illegitimacy was a badge of shame, not only to the mother but to the child. There are some fundamental differences here that could affect our society for decades ahead.

Twenty-six percent of all adults and teenagers alike, and slightly more women then men, say it's all right for a woman to bear children outside of marriage. And more than half of all college students think it's OK.

Jobs

Nowhere is the success of the women's movement more obvious than in the workplace. Younger women, better educated than any previous generation, are getting more of the skills they need to succeed; they have a wider feeling of choice and economic independence in their marriages and relationships.

The fact that a majority of the women in the USA work outside the home symbolizes a movement that will increase rapidly in the years ahead. When we surveyed teenagers, 82 percent of the girls said they expect to be working full time when they reach age 30—only 11 percent fewer than the boys. And only 11 percent of the girls said they expect to be staying home.

Government statistics show that by 1990, 65 percent of all new job applicants will be women. And, most importantly, women are making significant progress in professional fields once reserved exclusively for men. Almost 25 percent of the people in medical schools, and a third of law students, are women. The number of female managers has doubled since 1972, the Census Bureau reports, and more women are going into business for themselves.

Here are some traditionally male-dominated fields in which women are expected to make the most progress, according to projections from the National Planning Data Corporation:

Occupation	Women in field, 1980	Projected for 1990	Increase
Engineering	64,809	262,177	304%
Computer programming	98,957	308,128	211
Engineering technicians	158,072	310,563	96
Physicians	57,966	102,916	77
Data processing equipment repairs	3,932	6,758	71

About 86 percent of female teenagers say they expect to make a great amount of money some time in their lives, and 88 percent say they expect to be in a position where people work for them. Both responses are about the same as we got from the boys.

It's also clear that women are not working just because they need the money. Most say they would work even if they didn't have to.

For example, we asked adults: Would you continue to work

if you had enough money to maintain your current standard of living? There was no difference between the sexes. Exactly half of the women and half of the men said yes. Another 15 percent of the men and 12 percent of the women said they would continue to work full time but would change their jobs.

Only one in five women said they wouldn't work at all.

Although working can cause significant stress for women, working does have an interesting and seldom-discussed side effect that really helps relationships between the sexes. Working may very well help women better understand the pressures on the men in their lives—and, while we don't have the results to prove it, it may make men more understanding of women as well.

We asked this question of more than 1,500 men and women. The results are striking:

"Women who work are likely to be more understanding of the pressures on men than women who don't work." Do you agree?

	Total	Men	Women
Strongly agree	45%	40%	49%
Moderately agree	35	38	32
Moderately disagree	11	12	9
Strongly disagree	6	6	6

The overwhelming agreement by men should be heartening. As we'll discuss more thoroughly in the next chapter, it may show that men want more than ever to be able to talk to someone on an equal level—that while they may have a long way to go toward doing their share of the dishes or laundry, they nevertheless are looking for an equal partner, a confidante. In many ways, the new woman is helping men to find the new man.

There's one important area where women continue to lag behind—*money*.

Women like money just as much as men. Their desire to be financially well off equals their desire for a good family life, particularly among younger women.

Women's salaries have risen dramatically but there's still a significant wage gap with men, although some younger women, particularly in growth industries, are almost matching their male counterparts.

The 65 cents that women make for every dollar a man earns should rise to only 80 cents by the year 2000, according to some well-documented studies.

Superwoman Meets Reality

There are some often-mentioned theories behind the wage gap. Some believe that women fall behind when they take time off to have children. Others blame it on the fact that women lack seniority for top jobs; that they are only now working their way through middle management toward higher paying jobs.

We don't think those are the only reasons. Putting aside the real possibility that simple sexism is the main cause, it appears from our studies that the mingling of new expectations and old values also keep women from getting ahead.

Despite the wage inequality and whatever sexism may be behind it, despite the pressures of living up to the '80s image, women desperately want to get ahead.

But there are some real problems.

First, women may find it hard to compete with men simply because many can spend less time on the job.

When surveyed by USA TODAY, 25 percent of the men say work, including commuting, consumes 11 or more hours a day. Only 10 percent of women spend this much time on the job. Labor Department statistics show that women, on the average, spend fewer hours at full-time jobs than men do.

As we showed earlier, there's a simple reason for this: Women shoulder the bulk of the work in maintaining a home, a family, a relationship. This does not appear to be changing much, although younger men are more willing to help around the home. There's not much difference, obviously, between never-married men and women—but the vast majority of working people do have either a family, a steady relationship, or the responsibility for children from a failed marriage.

The fact that most household duties fall on women leads to the problem of finding a new balance between home and work. And the problem will continue—and likely grow—as more women enter the work force, for higher-level jobs with more demands. Women are simply moving into the office faster than men are taking up the slack at home.

Women are, however, just as likely as men to take work home with them: 36 percent take work home regularly. And when they do, women work an average of two hours and six minutes. Both these statistics are the same as for men.

"It's not hard if you don't mind not sleeping," said one professional businesswoman from Washington, D.C.

Many working women have other constraints as well.

More than half, 54 percent, say they couldn't spend more time away from home if they were offered a better job. Men don't feel that constraint nearly as much. Women are also 38 percent less likely than men to say they would move for a better job.

Moving—up and out—is a traditional path to better jobs and higher pay; and women more than men are cut off from this path.

Still, women derive more satisfaction from their jobs than men do: 56 percent say they are "very satisfied" with their jobs, a rating 14 percent higher than that of men and a finding confirmed by several national surveys we've done for USA TODAY.

And the satisfaction women get from work goes up substantially as they get older, as children get older, and as the demands from home decrease.

There are a few more interesting points we've found about women and work.

The man's job still seems to take precedence over his mate's. Men we've surveyed don't think that they should reduce their career goals if their mate takes a job. And women don't think the men should either.

But things are getting a little more equal on this front—our results show that both men and women are changing in their responses to this matter. They're both becoming a little more likely to give the woman's job equal weight to her mate's.

We think we'll see more of this as women achieve higher levels of job responsibility.

OK, so men and women don't think that a man should have to reduce his goals when his mate works. But in reality, does he pull back from his own expectations in order to accommodate a working woman?

That's not so clear.

Men are pretty much split on the issue. Women are less so; a majority say the man doesn't change when the woman goes to work.

We asked this question of 1,500 adults in a recent survey. The results:

"When a woman works, a man will have to reduce his own career goals." Do you agree?

	Total	Male	Female
Agree	42	45	38
Disagree	51	49	54
Not sure	7	6	8

A second interesting point involves the boss. Women, just as much as men (and in some ways more so) perpetuate the sexist notion that the boss should be a he instead of a she.

Only 39 percent of women say they would want to work for a woman boss. And women are 30 percent more likely than men to say they *strongly* want to work for a man instead of a woman. Again, this will be interesting to watch as women move in greater numbers up the career path.

Role Overload

So what's the impact of these pressures we've been discussing: work, home, motherhood? The changing role of women is having a direct impact on the stress felt by women and men.

A group of interesting ideas is developing in the '80s, the Image Age. One of them is that women and men should be liberated from the sex stereotypes of their mothers and fathers, their grandmothers and grandfathers.

We asked people whether they agree with this statement: "Life was simpler and more satisfying in the traditional family in which the man worked and the wife stayed home to raise children":

	Total	Male	Female
Strongly agree	29%	30%	28%
Moderately agree	22	25	20
Moderately disagree	23	25	22
Strongly disagree	20	17	24

The results are pretty well split. But one thing that stood out in the analysis: Single women and working women are the least likely to agree with the idea that the traditional setup was more "simple and satisfying."

One of the most positive effects of the women's movement is that it's given women more of a choice in what to do. But some are accepting the choice better than others, and not in the way you'd think.

In a massive survey on the relationships between the sexes, we asked thousands of men and women how "liberated" they considered themselves—for whatever meaning that word has for them. Here's how men and women viewed themselves:

	Total	Male	Female
Very liberated	31%	35%	27%
Somewhat liberated	53	50	56
Not very liberated	9	6	11
Not liberated at all	3	2	3

Surprisingly, it is the women who consider themselves only "somewhat liberated" that also reported higher levels of stress in all areas of their lives.

There was less stress on either side of them. Women who consider themselves very liberated, and those who consider themselves not liberated at all, reported much less stress in their lives.

Think about that for a second. In this age in which one's liberation (again, by whatever definition we have for ourselves) is so important to one's self-image, those on the opposite ends of the issue are just about equally satisfied with their lives.

It's the women caught in the middle—those who haven't really accepted or totally rejected the changing roles of women—who have the most trouble.

For example, women who considered themselves only "somewhat liberated" or "not very liberated"—the ones in the middle of the scale—were:

- 70 percent more likely than other women to cite problems communicating their feelings.
- 53 percent more likely to cite stress caused by disciplining their children.
- 40 percent more likely to cite worries about financial problems.
- 40 percent more likely to cite stress caused by their husbands' job demands.

Those are some pretty powerful differences. What's causing these women so much trouble?

Women who consider themselves "very liberated" have adopted the '80s image of the superwoman. They've matched the expectations of modern life, or at least tried to.

Women who consider themselves "not liberated at all" have made a conscious decision to stay with the traditional woman's lifestyle; in many cases the lifestyle of her mother. In both of these cases, the woman has for better or for worse found a set of ideals and decided for herself to stick to them.

The woman who considers herself only somewhat liberated is caught in a tug of war between the image and expectation of the '80s and the security of the traditional lifestyle. The result is an inner conflict.

Experts tell us this conflict can take the form of fatigue, anger, guilt, even depression—and can affect women either married or single. A USA TODAY survey of 982 psychiatrists showed that women are much more likely to be treated for depression than men are. But they're also more likely to admit their problems and seek help.

The liberation movement is affecting men also, but in a different way. Here, it's not the men in the middle who get caught.

Men who consider themselves "not liberated at all" are the ones who feel the most stress when it comes to dealing with women. Why is this different for men and women?

When a woman rejects the options of liberation, people view that decision as her own choice. Whether they agree or disagree, she gets moral support for her decision—even the staunchest liberationist will defend her right to make up her own mind. In fact, most will say that's the whole point of the movement in the first place.

But when a man rejects giving women more choices and opportunities, he's viewed as sexist, as an oppressor. He's somehow made himself part of the problem instead of part of the solution.

As we'll see in the next chapter, this conflict is part of the new pressures on men in the '80s. The conflict between trying to keep up a "macho" image while living up to the expectation of liberation is confusing and difficult. It's just one of a series of contradictions that men are trying to work out as they head through the decade.

CHAPTER FOUR

Men

In the early 1980s we discovered The New Man. He was sensitive. He was in tune with his feelings and the feelings of those around him. He wasn't afraid to show his emotions. Why, he'd even cry, if it came to that. He treated women as his equals; in fact, he wasn't quite sure he was equal to *them*. He looked a little like Alan Alda.

Then somewhere around the middle of the '80s we discovered, lo and behold, that Alan Alda had turned into Don Johnson. "Real men" were back. Sales of cigars and poker chips actually went up. Beer drinking was in; white wine was out. All the male stars suddenly had a five o'clock shadow.

Did our values really swing around that drastically?

Well, in a word, no. Neither of those images accurately reflects what men have wanted to be—or what women have wanted them to be—through the decade. The new man, in many ways, was a myth; and the new macho, in many ways, a caricature.

Clearly, it's more complicated to be a man now, in large part due to the emergence of women. For generations, men have defined their worth and masculinity largely through their jobs; for women the key role has been home and family. Little by little, though, men began seeing themselves pitted against women in the workplace, and realized they'd have to re-evaluate some priorities and goals.

No matter how liberated the male, he's finding more and more that his old definition of masculinity—based in the office and dedicated to the proposition that all *men* are created equal—is being challenged. Some men have taken to the challenge well, and some haven't; but the point is, all have had to face this challenge.

In 1950 more than 60 percent of households were headed by a male breadwinner with a wife at home full time. Today that's less than 10 percent. In 63 percent of the households with at least two adults, both adults work.

So what happened, beginning in the '60s, was this: Men started to become a little uneasy—and a little frustrated, since they really had no choice in the change. Women were in the active role when it came to changing the workplace. For the first time in their collective lives, men saw the workplace changing and couldn't do a thing about it.

The unease has continued and made life confusing for men in the '80s. Add to that the fact that men really don't turn to each other for help, as women do. Sisterhood is powerful, but brotherhood is harder to find. Women, coming from a place of oppression, know they need each other's help. Men, trying to hold on to a traditional power base, fear that showing a need for help can be seen as a sign of weakness.

So men haven't built the support groups, formal or informal, that women have. (Just for the record, since this is a much-debated topic, women in our surveys found making friends with another woman three times easier than making friends with a man. Men found male-bonding only a little easier than making friends with a member of the opposite sex.)

In addition, the changing role of the man has received much less attention, much less study, than has been paid to the changes among women.

What does that all add up to? Men thought they had to be Phil Donahue for a while, then they thought they had to be Mr. T. Or maybe both. They weren't sure how to talk to their buddies about it, and nobody was paying much serious attention to their problems anyhow.

What that added up to was this: Men began feeling pretty confused. Tough but sensitive, independent but needy, controlling but tolerant—confused.

The studies we've done involving men show that they're adapting to all this. They're changing in their attitudes toward women, relationships, work, and children. But not without an emotional cost.

New Roles, New Contradictions

For starters: Men are becoming uncertain about their new roles in society. Sixty-five percent of the USA's adults tell us that men today are confused about how to treat women. Among just single men, that figure is even higher: 74 percent of them say they are confused about how to treat women.

That's three out of four!

Imagine that. Three out of four men are confused about their roles in relationships with women. Things have sure changed a lot since the days of Humphrey Bogart.

Two things we've found. One: Men do want to be more open. They say they're looking for a relationship in which they can form a team with a woman—to be open and mutually supportive against the rigors of the world in which they both work and play. Two: At the same time, men are afraid of losing their masculinity.

What this results in: some interesting and surprising contradictions between what men do and what they *say* they do. Let's look at a few.

Contradiction No. 1: The importance of work

Men have long defined their masculinity by their ability to make a living, to be the breadwinner for the family. Now, however, more than 60 percent of wives work full time. With women sharing that burden, men tell us that work is less important now; they get less satisfaction from their jobs. They expect, and feel expected, to spend more time at home, helping maintain the home and raise the children. Indeed, this changing mood shows up in our research.

When we asked men, in several surveys, to rank the satisfaction they received from various parts of their lives—in what areas they feel "very satisfied"—the results were always the same. "Husband" and "father" always ranked at the top.

Here's the entire list:

Husband	32%
Father	25
Work or job	9
Being a son	8
Friend to women	8
Friend to men	4
Brother or sister	3
Not sure	11

As you can see, the satisfaction that men receive from their job is bunched with other bottom priorities, far behind the top two.

And when we turned the question around—asking what role they found the *least* satisfying—what came in No. 1? Work, well ahead of anything else.

Finally, what do men say causes them the most stress in their lives? Work, by far. This is particularly true of men whose wives also work.

OK. So men are finding that work is less and less the thing that fills their needs. It is nowhere near the thing that causes them the most satisfaction, but easily the thing that causes them the most stress.

So is this disenchantment reflected in the way men really live their lives? The answer is no.

First of all, men spend a heck of a lot more time being employees than they do being husbands and fathers. That's not on the wane—it's increasing. And that's not just for financial reasons, at least not directly. It's for ego reasons as well. Even though the family is what men believe is most important to them, it is still the workplace where they try to prove their masculinity and worth to themselves.

Among men working full time, 82 percent spend more than nine hours a day at work. And more than one in four males spend more than 11 hours a day at work.

Compare this to the amount of time men spend at home with their families. Half of all men—54 percent—spend only about 3.5 waking hours a day with their families.

Don't chalk that up to mere necessity: Women, even working women, spend far more time at home.

And what are men doing when they're at home? Watching television ranks No. 1.

And what do men think they do best? Be a good father? A good husband? Nope. When we asked men to tell us how they handled each area of their lives, work ranked No. 1 again.

Percent of men rating themselves as an excellent . . .	
Worker	54%
Father	47
Husband	39
Friend to women	39
Son	38
Friend to men	37

And, even more surprisingly, 54 percent of the men say it's likely they would uproot their families and move to another city if they were offered a better job. Among working women, only a third say they would move.

In fact, one marriage counselor told us that "men tend to seek therapy only when their *job* function (their 'doing') is in jeopardy. Women seek therapy in relation to the quality of their lives (their 'being')."

So there's Contradiction No. 1. The thing that men believe they do best is the thing that gives them the least satisfaction. Men get more enjoyment and satisfaction from their family, but devote the least time to it; and they believe the family is more important than the job, but they'd uproot the family if work demanded it.

Why is this?

Perhaps men are just starting to react to the changing role of women. As we'll see in the next chapter, many men are unsure about their roles in today's society. Perhaps their hearts are telling them where their priorities really should lie; but a hundred years of the American work ethic, generation after generation of men showing their stuff by bringing home the bacon, is not an image one can break simply because some doctor on a TV talk show says it's OK to be more sensitive now.

Contradiction No. 2—What men want in a woman
We did some in-depth follow-up interviews with a lot of the men in this next survey. The conversations kept coming back to the same theme: They wanted an open relationship with their mate. They wanted to have someone to tell their problems to, someone who'd be understanding and supportive. A partner in life.

In the survey, an overwhelming majority of men said they consider themselves "liberated" from sexual stereotypes. They say they're in favor of expanded roles for women; they lean toward equal rights in some form.

So, you would think that men would also want their wives to be liberated women, right?

Wrong!

Only 37 percent of men say a liberated women is a better marriage partner. More than half of all men disagree—53 percent say a liberated woman would *not* be a better marriage partner.

Now consider this (and remember, men overwhelmingly consider themselves "liberated"): We also asked if relationships between men and women improve when women become more independent.

Here are the results from men:

Yes	48%
No	47
Not sure	5

Statistically, that's an exact split. Our liberated men aren't sure whether they really want liberated women.

And look at this next table, too. We asked men if life will improve for them as women become more independent. The results:

Yes	45%
No	45
Not sure	10

Another tie!

These men who say they're liberated and in favor of equal

rights for women don't want a liberated mate, aren't sure if women's independence helps a relationship, and are exactly split on whether independence makes the world better for them.

When it comes to liberation, it's strictly, "Not with my wife you don't."

This contradiction—again, a contradiction between what men say and what they do—is another result of the Image Age.

Men's desire to consider themselves liberated is certainly a step forward, but it's also a result of doing what seems to be expected of them—not necessarily a real internal change but possibly a more superficial one.

They may have been very comfortable with their old values, but they ran full steam into the Image Age, when such seemingly inoffensive terms as "mankind" or "congressman" could make their date look at them as though they'd put ketchup on their tofu.

And that was the real conflict: Men may have been trying to act like the New Man, because it was the in thing to do. But real inner change, true liberation, comes much more slowly. And when the mid-'80s brought on yet *another* image to live up to—a fast-driving, hard-drinking, head-butting, hard-loving loser—that struggle became even tougher.

Maybe it's just that confusing times bring on a measure of nostalgia, and the uncertainty of the '80s is bringing the John Wayne in men back to the foreground—Rambo parachute-dropping out of the subconscious to do battle with Woody Allen.

This was the flip side of those in-depth interviews. While men said they wanted a supportive and equal mate, they were afraid of the humiliation that would come if it seemed they were anything less than confident and assertive. This may help to explain the contradiction between family and work. Faced with this conflict at home, men focus their attention on work. It's safer. And as long as they didn't call the women in their office "the girls," they didn't get in trouble.

Contradiction No. 3: A working wife
More than three out of four men—78 percent—say working

women are better able to understand the job pressures they're under.

But a majority say life is easier in a traditional family where the husband works and the wife stays home.

This contradiction isn't as hard to understand. Men have to do more around the home when women work. A full two-thirds of the USA's men say they're expected to take more responsibility around the home and spend less time at work when their mate has a job.

The key phrase here is "expected to"—because as we've already seen, they may be expected to do more work around the house, but they don't actually do that much more. So there's conflict and strife when they get off work and get into an argument over who should cook dinner, or stop off at the cleaners, or take the dog for a walk.

And that's not to mention the internal conflict we've already seen. Feeling they should be doing more work around the house means a fundamental reordering of the priorities they grew up with.

As we saw in the previous chapter, men are doing more work around the house, to a degree—but women tell us that men don't do as much as men think they do.

Here, by the way, is a good example of how Madison Avenue and the Real World feed each other, causing change and reflecting it as well. Men aren't doing nearly enough around the home, their mates say, but they are doing more than their fathers did. Advertisers recognize this subtle shift, and play to it, hoping to entice men to buy products never targeted for them before. Suddenly you see fewer commercials with clumsy men totally unable to do their own laundry until the woman next door comes to their rescue with a box of detergent. Little by little, you've seen—and will see more—ads for health care products and food and cleansers directed to men as well as to women. Madison Avenue hopes to sell products to men it has never sold to men before. And, as men buy more, Madison Avenue targets them even more, keeping the cycle going.

One last point—88 percent of men feel that when both parents have careers, men should be equally willing to make career sacrifices in order to share the responsibilities of raising children.

Again, what they say and what they do are very, very different. We've all read stories about men and women sharing jobs and splitting the household and child-rearing chores equally. But the reason we read news stories about these people is because they *are* news. There aren't many such stories around and there's little evidence that this is anything resembling a growing trend.

The Woman's Role

Women play an interesting part in keeping these contradictions going. While their desire to change the world is honest and sincere, they're not quite sure they want men to give up some of the traditional roles they've played.

And the traditional role of breadwinner is the one that causes the most conflict here.

Although most women consider themselves independent and liberated, they place no less importance than their mothers did on a man's ability to earn a living.

We asked first how women today rate the importance of a man's providing an adequate income to support his family. Specifically, we asked women: Do women in general put more value on it than they used to?

The results:

	Total	Male	Female
The same	59%	58%	60%
More value	16	18	14
Less value	19	19	19
Not sure	6	5	7

Older women say this, married women say this, even young single women say this.

Next we asked women: "Do you yourself place more or less value than your mother did on a man's ability to support his family?"

Here are the surprising results:

The same	62%
More value	15
Less value	18
Not sure	5

Even among the youngest females, 18-25, exactly half say they feel a man's ability to generate income is as important to them as it was to their mothers. A few said it was less important, about the same number as said it was more important.

This comes as a surprise, because you'd expect young, liberated women to say it's less important—that it's now much more likely, and acceptable, and possible, for the woman to be the breadwinner.

And this especially comes as a surprise to men, who are confused enough already.

So how about you? Where do you stand on all of this? Are you really as liberated as you think you are? Compare yourself to the people around you. Take this short test; then see how you stack up. Be honest.

	Yes	No
1. As women become more independent, things will actually improve for men.	☐	☐
2. Male and female relationships involve a lot more tension today than they used to.	☐	☐
3. A liberated women is likely to make a better marriage partner than a more traditional one.	☐	☐
4. Women don't seem to appreciate men as much as they used to.	☐	☐
5. Relationships will improve between men and women as a result of the increasing independence of women.	☐	☐
6. Men are increasingly confused about how they should treat women.	☐	☐
7. Today if a man marries a woman who works, he had better expect to spend a lot more time on family responsibilities and less on his job.	☐	☐
8. A man's ability to earn a good income to support his family is as important as it ever was.	☐	☐
9. Working women are better able to understand their mates' job pressures than women who don't work.	☐	☐
10. When both parents have careers, men should be equally willing to make career sacrifices.	☐	☐

Here are the responses from men and women (percent agreeing):

Question 1: As women grow more independent, things improve for men.

Men	48%
Women	47%

Question 2: Relationships involve more tension.

Men	77%
Women	79%

Question 3: Liberated women make better marriage partners.

Men	38%
Women	38%

**Question 4: Women don't appreciate men
as much as they used to.**

Men	41%
Women	45%

**Question 5: Relationships will improve between
men and women as women become more independent.**

Men	48%
Women	47%

**Question 6: Men are increasingly confused about how
to treat women.**

Men	65%
Women	69%

**Question 7: If a man marries a working women,
he'd better plan on spending more time on family
responsibilities and less on the job.**

Men	67%
Women	56%

**Question 8: A man's ability to earn a good income
is just as important as it ever was. (WOMEN ONLY)**

Same	62%
More important	15%
Less important	17%

**Question 9: Working women are better able
to understand their mates' job pressures.**

Men	78%
Women	81%

**Question 10: When both parents have careers,
they should be equally willing to make career sacrifices.**

Men	45%
Women	37%

So there you are: the conflicts women face in the '80s, and the problems men face.

When they get together, though, the sparks *really* fly.

CHAPTER FIVE

Battle of the Sexes

Enough about men and women—now let's talk about sex.

The war between men and women, James Thurber would be glad to know, rages on through the '80s, though it has taken some twists and turns even he never counted on.

First, the foreplay. What attracts us to each other? Well, no great surprise here. Beauty may be only skin deep, but here in the Image Age we go in for deep skin. Maybe in the '60s a guy could pick up a woman by stroking his beard, passing the joint, hooking a thumb through the strap of his tattered OshKosh B'Gosh overalls while quoting T.S. Eliot—but back here in the future it's personality first, looks second, and everything else trailing behind. It's the women in the *New York Times Magazine* ads, not the ones who wrote the articles, who top the list.

Looks and personality are where it's at in the '80s. Sad but, from our poll results, true: Look somewhere down the list and you'll find those minor qualities such as intelligence and honesty running neck-and-neck with a nice smile and a good wardrobe.

What attracts you to someone of the opposite sex?

Men say:		Women say:	
Personality	20%	Personality	22%
Looks	20	Looks	17

Figure	11	Sense of humor	13
Sense of humor	9	Eyes	10
Intelligence	9	Honesty	10
Honesty	7	Intelligence	9
Eyes	7	Smile	6
Smile	7	Dress	6
Dress	5	Figure	4
Hair	3	Hair	1

When we asked the same questions of teens, looks easily placed first, thanks mostly to teenage boys. Half said appearance is the most important thing about a girl.

Girls say their first consideration is consideration. They want their young men first and foremost to be kind and considerate. (Note, by the way, that "kind and considerate" wasn't mentioned by enough adults—men or women—to even make the chart.) For teenage girls, looks place a close second.

This emphasis men place on appearance, going back to the early teens, is perhaps one reason that more women than men don't like what they see in the mirror.

Consider these results from USA TODAY polls:

- 54 percent of the nation's adult men are satisfied with the way they look. Only a third of all women like their own looks.
- 61 percent of all women say they need to lose weight compared with 45 percent of all men.
- Women are much more likely than men to say they need regular exercise.

In fact, for three years in a row we asked people to tell us what they hope to achieve in the coming year. Topping the list overall was exercise—72 percent said they want more exercise. But the difference between the sexes was noticeable—76 percent for women, 68 percent of the men.

When it came to losing weight, the difference was even greater. Many more women than men—61 percent to 45 percent—want to lose weight in the coming year.

And when we asked about New Year's resolutions we again found men and women setting very different kinds of goals.

Here's a look at how men and women differ in their New Year's resolutions:

- 50 percent of men want to work harder on the job, compared with 45 percent of women.
- Men are more likely—51 percent to 44 percent—to want to get a medical checkup. But women are more likely to go out and get one.
- Men are more likely to want to spend more time with their families, 65 percent to 60 percent, but women are more likely to do it.

But don't take that the wrong way. Overall, women are more likely to make New Year's resolutions, but the sexes are equally likely to keep them.

Turnoffs

Nobility of spirit, concern for one's fellow man, kindness to puppies, depth of soul—who needs 'em here in the Image Age? Men are more turned off by a loud voice than by a dishonest woman. In other words, go ahead and lie; just be quiet about it.

Well, maybe men haven't become as crass as all that—but when we asked people their turnoffs, here's what topped the list:

Men: What turns you off about a woman?	
Overweight women	52%
Unkempt appearance	40
Sour disposition	39
Loud voice	35
Too much makeup or perfume	29

Women, on the other hand, don't mind 'em large—just as long as they're neat and sweet about it. Your turn:

Women: What turns you off about a man?	
Sloppy men	64%
Sour disposition	54
Overweight	45
Appearing conceited	40
Loud voice	35

Our Idols

There was a time when people like Woody Allen used to show up on "sexiest man in America" polls. But our tastes have gotten a little bit more predictable.

Together with "PM Magazine," the nationally syndicated evening entertainment show, we asked a series of questions about the USA's favorites.

Who is the sexiest man on television?

Hawaii's sexy, self-deprecating, sometimes bumbling private investigator, Tom Selleck—Magnum PI—easily ranked No. 1 when we asked this question of women (remember, looks and personality are the key these days). In fact, Selleck doubled the number of votes received by his closest pursuer, the fashion plate of "Miami Vice," Don "Sonny Crockett" Johnson. Here are the top choices among the 142 men mentioned:

Thomas Magnum (Tom Selleck)	30%
Sonny Crockett (Don Johnson)	14
Ricardo Tubbs (Philip Michael Thomas)	3
Blake Carrington (John Forsythe)	3

In fact, Selleck was also rated as the sexiest man in all of entertainment, easily defeating Robert Redford, Don Johnson, and Burt Reynolds.

Who is the sexiest man in all of entertainment?

Tom Selleck	32%
Robert Redford	20
Don Johnson	14
Burt Reynolds	14
Sylvester Stallone	11
Philip Michael Thomas	3

Who is the sexiest woman on television?

Forget about those 18-year-old starlets. The average age of the four sexiest women on TV is almost 42. Here they are:

Krystle Colby (Linda Evans), age 43	10%
Alexis Colby (Joan Collins), age 52	6
Maddie Hayes (Cybill Shepherd), age 36	4
Pam Ewing (Victoria Principal), age 36	4

Who is the sexiest woman in all of entertainment?

Linda Evans	19%
Loni Anderson	15
Joan Collins	15
Morgan Fairchild	14
Cybill Shepherd	11
Madonna	10
Diahann Carroll	8

Some Deeper Values

Good news! There is in fact some indication that we haven't gone totally off the shallow end. When we asked what upset people most in their closest personal relationships, it wasn't that their partner was getting thick around the waist or thin around the hairline. Solid relationship goals—honesty, openness, spending time together—all began to surface. And there was almost no difference between men and women in their answers. Here are the results:

What upsets you most in your closest personal relationship?	
Dishonesty	19%
Lack of communication	14
Too little time together	11
Arguments	10
Inconsiderate behavior	10
Money	10
Lateness	9
Nagging	8
Infidelity	4

There's an interesting difference between men and women on this subject, however. When we asked people what they'd

like their main squeeze to do less, men were more likely than
women to say "smoking"; women were much more likely
than men to say "drinking."

What would you like your mate to do less of?			
Activity	Total	Men	Women
Smoking	20%	23%	16%
Arguing	11	14	8
Drinking	9	4	13
Eating too much	9	9	9
Being late	9	8	11
Spending too much time away from home	8	6	9
Spending too much money	8	11	4

The Real Thing

OK, enough beating around the bush. Now we know what
turns you on and who turns you on. So, how's your sex life?

For the most part, almost everyone said, "No problem."
And 93 percent say it's just as good as or getting better than it
was a year ago (25 percent, "getting better"; 68 percent, "the
same.") Only 4 percent say it's getting worse.

The War Between Men and Women

But beneath the surface—behind the USA's apparent preoc-
cupation with looks, behind the simple answers to a simple
question about our sex life—lie some real problems between
men and women here in the Image Age.

As we've seen before, living up to the Image Age is not
without its problems.

Things may be OK in the sack, but once we put our clothes
on and try to have an intelligent conversation, once we put on
our power suits and try to compete for jobs, once we carpool
to the office with our mate and try to share experiences on the
ride home, something goes amiss.

Men and women are trying to adjust to the enormous social
changes we've discussed in the last two chapters. And the
more their lifestyles—particularly their work lifestyles—

resemble each other's, the more trouble they have talking to each other.

Here's how it goes: More women are working (we already know that). The more women work, the more men's former power base is eroded.

But it's not just a matter of how liberal, or how liberated, or how threatened a man feels by that. Money changes everything. Couples in which both partners are working are much more likely to share in the big decisions and the little ones: how much to spend on a car or a home, how much to save, invest, spend on insurance.

So both partners are wearing the pants in the family—and what results is a blurring of sex roles. That can be terrific, if the couple can handle it; it can lead to the true partnership that people of both sexes at least *think* they really want.

But the surveys show that more often, the blurring leads to a backlash—and both men and women have difficulty handling the fallout.

When we asked people to rate relationships between men and women today, more than three out of four—a full 77 percent of men and 79 percent of women—said relationships between the sexes involve a lot more tension than in previous years. And it didn't make any difference whether the person was young or old, single or married.

The source of the problem, it appears, is more on the man's side. He's confused about how to treat women these days.

We asked thousands of men and women about relationships between the sexes; 65 percent of the men said they're confused about how to treat women, and 69 percent of the women agreed.

This cut across all age groups:

- 62 percent of all married people said so.
- 73 percent of singles said so.
- 78 percent of all divorcees said so.

The Game of Love

What are the ramifications of all this? A recent USA TODAY survey of almost 1,000 psychiatrists, psychologists, social workers, and marriage counselors gives us some hints.

For starters, we asked: What are the main reasons that people seek psychiatric help in the '80s? Problems with intimate relationships rank first, for married adults and for single adults.

Here are some comments from the mental health workers surveyed:

- A Pittsburgh social worker: "Women don't know what they are 'supposed to' think, feel, or do. Men are confused by women."

- A New Haven, Conn., social worker: "Women are more confused about their roles and have fewer clear role models. This results in more anxiety, greater feelings of helplessness, false strivings, gender confusion, and often in eating disorders."

- A Boston psychologist: "Many women now are struggling with the conflicts between the pressures of newly accepted roles and older, more traditional claims on their feminine identity. Men are struggling with issues regarding the sharing of power while struggling to maintain their masculine identity."

- A Kansas psychiatrist: "Men and women are struggling with the change in sex roles; men in giving up power and becoming vulnerable and women with accepting power and taking responsibility for themselves."

- A New York psychologist and university professor: "Women continue to be 'trained,' raised in a traditional feminine manner, then expected to function as a 'liberated woman.' Lacking proper preparation, they often behave like castrated, unhappy men. Men continue to be taught to hold back their emotions, and then become confused when they are unable to have any deep relationships."

- An Olympia, Wash., psychiatrist: "Men are not taught to accept dependency gracefully, while women are not taught to assume autonomy with dignity."

- A Dallas psychiatrist: "Females struggle with feeling OK about being strong and assertive—and handle the load of feeling they're the 'only one in the family noticing the problems.' Men are confused about what women are going through; they feel very inadequate in relationships, and make up for the resulting feelings of inadequacy by being 'more successful' at work."

■ A San Francisco family counselor: "Women are increasingly feeling their internal power, but are frustrated about how to influence the 'externals'—how to resolve male/female relationships. Men are frightened by them; they feel pushed and unsure of their next move, and need to redefine their roles."

Finally, a reference from a Houston psychiatrist points to the problems created by expectations of the Image Age:

"Many patients of both sexes are severely stressed by the changing sex roles they feel are being imposed on them by culture and the media."

Indeed, a full 40 percent of the psychiatrists and psychologists responding to our survey said many of their patients are confused about sex roles today, making this a growing neurosis of the '80s. And more than a third say patients complain about dissatisfaction with their sex lives.

About three out of four, 76 percent, say they've seen major changes in the mental health of their patients over the past 10 years. And 68 percent say there are differences in the mental health problems between men and women. The problem cited most often: people unable to keep up with the change in sex roles—cited by exactly one-third of the mental health experts.

This kind of confusion is evident from a series of questions we asked of 1,500 adults. Men are confused about how they're supposed to act: They think they should be more open, but also think that "being more open" means "acting more like a woman." And they are pretty sure they're *not* supposed to do that.

First, we asked: Do women want men to be more open? A vast majority—90 percent of men, 90 percent of women — said yes.

Then we asked: Do women want men to behave more like women? The results were very different—24 percent of men said yes; 13 percent of women said yes.

One result of the confusion is that men aren't sure whether women appreciate them. Look at the results of this next question—with the results almost evenly split:

"Women don't appreciate men as much as they used to." Do you agree?

	Agree	Disagree
Men	41	49
Women	45	49

The Problems That Problems Cause

Finally, we asked the mental health experts how they see the effects of all these problems. They said that among men, the result is greater use of drugs and alcohol. Among women, depression is a major result.

Explains a California psychologist and marriage counselor: "Women 'act in'; they blame and punish themselves. Eating disorders, depression and agoraphobia (the fear of being in public places) all strike many more women than men; and all represent psychic energy turned inward. Men 'act out.'"

Men are less likely to seek help than are women. And, the experts told us, they are more likely to be violent.

The Real Gender Gap

There's another, more quantitative reason that women are a little uptight about their sex roles. In longer, in-depth interviews, they tell us there simply aren't enough good men out there. Statistics indicate this is no idle concern. One out of five women today has no potential mate because there are simply not enough men to go around.

Overall, there are 94.5 men in the USA for each 100 women. Here's a look at states with the fewest men per 100 women:

Area	Men per 100 Women
District of Columbia	86.1
New York	90.5
Massachusetts	90.8
Rhode Island	90.0
Pennsylvania	91.9

In the 30-to-34 age group, there are actually 102 women for every 100 men. This changes to 128-to-100 by age 35 and 135-women-to-100-men by age 40.

That last age group is the toughest for women because many of those men are divorced. They often remarry younger women.

Take that all into account, and it becomes really difficult for women in their 40s to find available, single men.

No Pressure

With all these problems out there in the world, why are parents always pushing their kids to get married?

Actually, they're not. Only 9 percent of singles say mom or dad push them toward matrimony, and that's the same for men and women.

In fact, although the vast majority of people—over 80 percent—*do* plan to get married some day, one of the major changes in our society over the past 10 years is that people now have the choice *not* to get married. Men and women are no longer looked upon as odd if they haven't married, as was the case a generation ago.

When we asked about this recently, 74 percent of all adults—76 percent of the men and 73 percent of the women— said it's fine nowadays if someone simply chooses not to marry. Even in the more conservative South, 70 percent agree it's OK not to marry. And, as we mentioned earlier, more people are also saying it's all right for a single woman to have a child.

The Last Myth

Well, that covers most of the battle of the sexes, but we all know there's one more thing that men and women fight about all the time.

And, as you might have guessed by now, it's based on a myth.

We're talking, of course, about women drivers.

Who are the USA's worst drivers? Men, not women. According to a USA TODAY study, men are:

- 73 percent more likely to get a speeding ticket
- 80 percent more likely to have a moving violation
- 300 percent more likely to get a parking ticket
- 50 percent more likely to be arrested for driving while intoxicated
- 24 percent more likely to have had an accident in the last five years.

CHAPTER SIX

Family Life

Do you take this man, this woman, in the bonds of holy matrimony? To love? Honor? Cherish? Obey? Forsaking all others? In sickness and in health?

Well, believe it or not, for the most part you do.

The demise of the traditional family has been widely reported. And much of what you've read has been quite accurate.

But there's something hiding behind the statistics that is quite surprising—something that tells us that the family isn't dying out at all.

It is true that the traditional, "Ward I'm Worried About the Beaver" family—a husband who works, a wife who stays home, and two or more children—accounts for less than 5 percent of all households.

And it's true that both mates work in 62 percent of all households. And that the numbers of non-relatives living together has increased 41 percent since 1970. And that almost half of all new marriages this year will likely end in divorce.

All of these statistics, when put together, paint a fairly grim picture. And the conclusion that's been drawn from them, although inaccurate, is understandable. It seems as though people are moving away from family life, that we have begun a trend that will signal the end of the family's dominance as a way of life in the USA.

We've seen that baby boomer women are delaying child-birth. The Census Bureau, early in 1986, said it was possible that 20 to 25 percent of all those born in the 1960s would live their lives childless. That would be an all-time record—beating out the 23 percent during the Depression.

The Census Bureau noted that was just conjecture, although it does fit into the image of the family falling apart as a main way of life in the USA.

But there is one thing we can be sure of from our USA TODAY studies: There is clearly a countercurrent, a force running in exactly the opposite direction from those Demise-of-the-Family projections.

And that is: Family life makes us happy. It always did. It still does. It makes us happier than just about anything else. It isn't waning. It isn't dying. In fact, as times get harder, the nurturing nest of family life may be becoming more important to people.

Married people are easily the happiest people in the USA, followed by singles. Divorcees are far behind.

Here's a look at people who say they are "very happy" with life:

Married	73%
Single	52
Divorced/separated	41
Divorced/with children	40

Don't let the burgeoning divorce rate fool you into thinking that marriage is on the way out. Divorce is the end of a living arrangement, but not the end of the needs and desires that brought us into that arrangement. Divorce signals unhappiness with an individual, not with the institution of marriage itself. Think about this: More than two-thirds of all divorcees remarry, more men than women and many within three years of their breakup.

There are two reasons that divorce may be increasing despite our unwavering desire to be married. One: Divorce has, in most segments of society, become more widely accepted, so the social pressure to stay in a bad marriage is much less of a factor in people's decisions.

The other has to do with the Image Age. The expectation

that people can—and should—have a "perfect marriage" leads to greater disappointment when the realities of daily life show up, and the marriage is anything less than perfect.

So people may be less willing to, or feel less pressured to, stay in a marriage that doesn't fulfill their expectations. But when they look elsewhere for the emotional support and intimacy they desire, the place they look is usually to another marriage.

The USA family has felt the full impact of the changes that have affected our society since the 1950s, the kinds of changes we've been talking about all through this book—the pressures of the Image Age, the changes in sex roles, the increase in women working, the push to take control of one's own life.

So rather than ask what's wrong with the family, a more relevant question may be: How has it remained so stable in light of all these changes? Because that's what really has been happening in the 1980s: The family has adapted to the changing roles of women, the changing expectations of men, the changing face of the battle between the sexes. The family isn't dying. It's just changing with the times.

We're Happy with Our Family Lives

Rich people and poor people and young people and old people have told us, in thousands of interviews, that their families are the most important parts of their lives. Indeed, the results of our surveys show that those people who say family values are dead are simply dead wrong. Consider:

- More than three out of four of us, 79 percent, say we are very satisfied with our families.
- 61 percent of all households gather together every night for dinner.
- More than one in four of us, 28 percent, help our parents financially.
- 66 percent would turn a job down if it meant spending more time away from our homes and families.
- 78 percent look forward to large, traditional family gatherings.

Adults today also believe they're more affectionate with their children than their parents were with them; that they're closer to their children than their parents were to them.

We also asked people to describe their relationship with their mate. The answers reflect what we cherish, want, and, indeed, expect from our relationships. More than three out of four, 78 percent, describe their relationship as warm and loving.

Other answers:

Peaceful coexistence	13%
Serious problems	8

And how important are our families to us? Consider this next question, which men and women answered in pretty much the same way:

What are you most satisfied with in your life?	
Your children	82%
Relationship with your spouse	81
Your family	79
Your friendships	74
Your health	64

The Children's Hour

It's true that people are having children later. In 1970, for example, women 30 and older had 18 percent of the USA's babies; by 1982 it was up to 22 percent.

Women are clearly delaying having children—sometimes delaying so long that, as the Census Bureau showed, they may never get around to it. But that doesn't necessarily signal a shift in women's values. Only 11 percent of the women in their late 20s and early 30s say they *plan* to remain childless, although the *real* percentage will probably be higher.

The vast majority of parents, 77 percent, tell us that their marriages are happier now than before they had children. Only 4 percent say they were happier without kids.

Why this apparent contradiction? Why are we having fewer children than we say we plan to? Why are we delaying childbirth if our desire to be parents isn't diminishing?

The answer, we think, may be part of the tricky game we

play here in the Image Age. In trying to Have It All, we sometimes lose the thing we care most about. Delaying children to start a career may seem like a sensible move, but fears grow as people see the sands running out on their "biological clocks"—real or imagined timetables for starting a family. Those fears create a climate of stress, a climate that some of us never climb out of.

On the other hand, there's one mighty realistic reason to delay having children until your career is well under way. Kids have gotten a lot more expensive than they used to be.

A recent Urban Institute study predicts it will cost an average of $142,700 to raise a child who is three years old today. And that doesn't include the cost of a college education, so add another $50,000 to $150,000, depending on what kind of school the child goes to.

But that's not stopping us, either. We still want to have children, because they provide a closeness we so desperately seek.

We noted earlier that when we asked a large cross-section of teenagers whom they feel closer to—mom or dad—mother won. Even the boys were twice as likely to say it's their mother they feel closer to. But both men and women say they feel closer to their children than their parents were to them at about the same age.

Now, we'd better stop for a second before we offend a lot of grandparents. It's very possible that people answer that way because it's natural to want to see yourself as a better parent than your parent was.

What's important here, though, is the perception of closeness. We feel close to our children, perhaps, because we want to feel close to them, because our need to feel close to them is so important, because they are so important to our lives. Kids mean so much to us.

Kids mean so much to us that when the '80s make us act in ways that run contrary to our feelings—spending too much time at work, for example—we feel terribly guilty. We'll talk more about this, but here's one quick indication that we're trying to make up for acting like busy '80s parents despite our home-and-hearth '50s values: A third of all parents say they buy too many toys for their children.

This may or may not be a way of trying to buy back their affection, but guess who's most likely to feel this way? Men at midcareer—those most likely to spend more time with their work and less with their children.

What Families Do Together

Some things never change. As we mentioned earlier, almost two-thirds of all families sit down together and have dinner just about every night. Another 23 percent of the families sit down and eat as a group at least three times a week.

And what do they do at dinner? Sit and talk, just like the old days. They talk about how school was today; in fact, that's the major topic of conversation. They talk about friends, and argue about politics, and tell jokes that the others have heard before, and enjoy each other's company.

More than three out of four teenagers surveyed in an extensive USA TODAY poll say they sit and talk with their parents when they have dinner together.

This might be more important than you think. A recent study conducted by several major universities shows an important link between these dinnertime talks and the success children have in school. And the longer and more involved are these conversations between parents and children, the more likely the kids are to do better in school.

It's clear that dinnertime is still a main focus of family life, which is why the rites and traditions of this meal seem to be remaining largely untouched. It's the other meals of the day that have changed much more as a result of the back-to-work movement of today's mothers. More than half of the teenagers—even the youngest among them—make their own breakfast. More than a third make their own lunch. Dad and mom do the same, by the way.

In fact, the National Restaurant Association reports that restaurants in 1983 saw a 2 percent jump in total business—but that the breakfast business rose 11 percent at the same time.

But mom still makes dinner, and that's usually the first time the family all gets together. (By the way, in case you were wondering: When we eat at home, about 51 percent of the time mom makes something fresh; 18 percent of the time we eat leftovers, 14 percent, sandwiches. About one night in nine, somebody brings home fast food.)

Of course, this culinary bastion of family life hasn't escaped the changes of the '80s *totally* unscathed. There is one thing that has changed about dinnertime: More often, we're doing it on the road.

According to one study, more than 41 cents of each dollar spent on food is spent on going out to eat—compared with 33 cents in the 1970s.

And the results of a USA TODAY study show that 63 percent of all familes go out to eat with the kids at least once a week; 81 percent eat out at least once a month.

Never fear, though—romance hasn't died. More than one in four couples with children leave the kids at home and have a nice dinner out at least once a week. And 65 percent dine sans children at least once a month.

This shift in our dinner habits—and again, it's more a tremor than an earthquake—can be attributed to a number of things.

Obviously, the soaring number of working women has a lot to do with it. With both the man and woman working in so many couples, they tell us it's sometimes faster and easier simply to go out.

Another reason surfaces, however, in follow-up in-depth interviews. After a hard day, it's simply nice to be waited on for a change. Also, and perhaps more important, there are more demands on the time that a family has together. Dining out gives them a chance to sit and talk without interruptions. When both mom and pop work, dinner is frequently prepared on deadline, and getting it on the table cuts into that valuable "How was school?" talk.

What else do families do together? Well, we're not so sure we're pleased to report this, but the absolute No. 1 family activity is tube watching.

You got it: A full 25 percent of the USA's households say that outside of eating, watching TV is the activity the entire family does together most frequently. Here are the figures:

What do you do most frequently with your family?	
Watch television	25%
Participate in sports	21

Shop	15
Sit and talk	13
Visit relatives	10

Perhaps even more surprising (or disappointing) is the amount of television that we watch: 28 percent of families say they watch three or more hours of television each night as a group. It's so important to us that we keep buying more sets—there are about 2.5 TV sets per household in the USA now, and that's expected to rise to 3 sets per home by the end of this decade.

Remember, those studies that show televisions are on in most homes an average of seven hours each day include a lot of "unattended TV." It's on, but nobody's watching.

What do men and women do together when the kids aren't around? Surprisingly, sports and recreation came in first—thanks mostly to their popularity among those under age 35. Television came in a comfortable second.

We asked married people (with and without kids):

What do you and your spouse do together most often when it's just the two of you?	
Sports or recreation	38%
Watch television	23
Go out to eat or drink	17
Do household chores	16
Shop	13
Go to movies	12
Sit and talk	10
Go for a walk	7
Go for a drive	6
Play cards or games	5

The Boys' Night Out is a myth. Although men are more likely to go out alone than women are, half of all adults—men and women alike—say they rarely, if ever, go out at night without their mate. Only 15 percent go out even once a week. When they do go out, men are more likely than women to visit bars or nightclubs, or to play sports. Women are more likely than men to go to meetings or classes of some kind; they're also more likely to shop or go to the movies.

Where do you go when you go out alone?			
Place	Total	Men	Women
Bars	31%	37%	25%
Play sports	19	30	8
Meetings or classes	16	12	21
Visit a friend	11	11	12
Shop	8	1	16
Go to the movies	7	2	12

So that's the overview of the family in the 1980s: stable, but changing; under siege, but adapting. More than anything else, surviving. Now let's take a quick look at some of the things families are doing—and how they're doing them.

Who Runs the Home

The nation's men may never forgive us for this section. But here it is. We asked this one over the course of three surveys. We conducted over 4,500 interviews. We asked men and women. We asked married people and we asked unmarried couples living together. We asked: Who is responsible for what decisions around the home?

The answers:

Women are responsible for:

- Deciding what's for dinner and then preparing it
- Managing the household budget
- Raising the children

Men and women share the responsibilities for deciding:

- Where to go on vacation
- Where to go when they eat out
- How much to spend on major purchases
- How much to save
- How much insurance to carry and where to buy it
- Where to invest savings

Men are responsible for deciding:

- What to watch on television

That's *it*? That's it. Virtually all other decisions are made jointly or made by the woman. Really.

The Extended Family

We've been talking so far mostly about the immediate family, but there's also a lot of evidence that we're still very close to our extended families—grandma and grandpa, aunts and uncles, cousins and brothers and sisters. There is no question that our new, mobile society has broken up the generations. We're a nation on the move and much, much more likely to live a day's drive from our parents than anyone ever was before.

This isn't likely to diminish, either. Families will continue to be more widespread across the nation; 58 percent of our teens say it's unlikely they'll be living in the same community as their parents by age 30. A third say they expect to live more than 200 miles away from home.

But our relations with grandpa and grandma and Uncle Arthur and Aunt Dorothy are important to us. They provide an anchor, a security blanket to help buffer us against the bumps and bruises of life. Consider large family gatherings—those occasions with 10 adults and 25 children and lots to eat and even more to drink and a dozen embarrassing questions all played against a background of more noise than you have encountered since you sat through a sudden death period at the football stadium.

Guess what? You love 'em. You can't wait to get there.

What reason do people give for this attachment? Well, there are a number of reasons. Two stand out: These gatherings are a link to the past, and something to look forward to for the future.

The vast majority, 78 percent of us, say we look forward to these family events. Only 5 percent find these gatherings stressful and say they would just as soon not go.

And, of course, Christmas is at the top of the list. Here's what people say:

Which family gatherings do you look forward to most?	
Christmas	60%
Thanksgiving	13
Family reunions	10

July 4	3
Other	14

There's one other interesting, significant way that the connections between us and our extended families show up. We still support each other, just as we always have, in the way that is sometimes the most important. When times are tough and we need some dough, it's our family that comes to the rescue.

People today are just as likely as in the past to give financial help to their loved ones; 28 percent say they have helped support their parents at some time. And 25 percent say they have received financial help from their parents sometime during their lives, other than for their own education. And to kill one more myth: Only 29 percent of those who received financial help said their parents wanted to know what the money was going to be used for. And only one in 14 said their parents seem to feel the loan gave them more to say about how they lived their lives.

Serious Problems

Of course, all is not sweetness and light in the family. We're not *always* having nice chats around the dinner table and heading off for a family evening in front of the TV.

Anyone who's ever been in a serious relationship knows that one activity is probably unavoidable: The Argument.

This might be something you'd want to remember next time you're having it out with your mate: The emotional release may be necessary, but keep it in perspective because 51 percent of both men and women say there's no winner or loser when they argue.

OK, you say, but when there *is* a winner, who wins? Well, we asked men and women this same question. They both had the same response; they win half of the fights and their mates win the other half.

Well, if that's the case, what are we arguing about?

As it turns out, we're arguing about the same things our parents argued about. Money tops the list, just as it has for decades.

Here's what married couples argue about:	
Financial matters	53%
Job demands	50
Disciplining children	50
Demands of spouse's job	47
Use of free time	42
Relatives	41
Household chores	40
Friends	32
Vacation	26
Children's education	24

So is money the root of all evil (or at least 53 percent of all evil)? No. These are the things we argue about, but these are not necessarily the cause of our serious problems. Even though money may be the first thing we find to argue about, most adults feel that poor communication causes almost *twice* as many problems as their finances. Not seeing each other enough and not doing enough things together are just as disruptive as not having enough money.

What causes you problems in your relationships?	
Poor communication	22%
Don't see each other	12
Money	12
Don't do enough together	12
Arguing	9
Messiness	9

In an earlier chapter, we talked about how men at least say they like it when their wife works. Their reason: They felt it made both partners understand the pressures each other was facing.

Well, here's something to indicate that they just might have been right.

When both adults work full time, they are less likely to argue about job demands, even though those demands usually put more of a strain on the marriage.

Men, however, are more likely than working women to cite

their own job demands as a reason for problems—further proof that men still place greater importance on their work than do women.

Teenagers

The subject of arguing seems to be a good time to turn our attention to those members of the family who eat everything in sight and blast us out of the house with loud music that we can't understand the lyrics to—teenagers.

What do we really argue about with our kids? Some serious stuff, some not-so-serious stuff. Tied for first are behavior and household chores.

Here are the top reasons we argue with our children:	
Behavior	24%
Household chores	24
School grades	12
Homework	12
Bedtime	7
Curfews	4
Arguing with siblings	4
Other	13

The rarity of arguing about curfew was surprising, since most kids—77 percent—still have curfews (the average for all teens: 10 P.M. on school nights and 12:30 on weekends). Kids still get grounded when they misbehave; 50 percent say they're not allowed out on weekends as a form of punishment. Next most common punishment: yelling.

Here's what kids say happens when they're bad:	
Grounded on weekends	50%
Yelling	19
Lose privileges	11
Talk things over with parents	6
No television	5
Strict curfew	4
Spanking	3

Extra chores	2
Lose allowance	2

We're taking a chance on starting another family argument here, but just for the record: Less than half (40 percent) of the USA's teens get an allowance. Almost 59 percent of those 13 to 14 get allowances; the percentage drops as kids get older and are more likely to have a job.

The questions we've been talking about so far concerning teenagers have been fairly simple, but many of the questions we've raised in our surveys about teenagers haven't been so easy.

Today's teens are a tough group to figure. Their music is eclectic—ranging across the board from hard-driving new wave to syrupy love songs. Their values are hard to pin down, and depending on the question, they sometimes seem more optimistic and sometimes much more pessimistic than the generations before them.

Their hopes, goals, fears, and desires vary widely between boys and girls, between rich kids and poor kids, between younger and older teenagers.

In general, our extensive survey of teenagers paints a portrait of USA teenagers as more home-oriented, more traditional, and less challenging of authority than in the past. Our survey also indicates that a growing resource will continue to prosper and flower: Clearly, today's teenage women will build on the progress and growth of their older sisters.

Above all else, it's important to realize that the USA's teens enjoy who they are, and where they are. An incredible 98 percent say they are happy; 56 percent say they are very happy. There's no easy way to reconcile this with the large numbers who fear that they will die in a nuclear war; no way to make this jibe with the growing problems of teenage suicide and drug abuse.

There may be no more telling feature of the teenage psyche in the 1980s than to consider this contradiction: They are not sure the world will have a future, and yet somehow, through some magic teenager understanding, they believe that the future will be bright.

Old Values

These teens, more than any of their rebellious predecessors in the last few decades, believe strongly in the traditional values their parents believe in.

When we asked teens what they are proudest of in their lives, "home and family" topped the list, followed by their own educational achievements and—brace yourself—"being an American." That's right; my home, my school, my country.

Ninety-two percent say they expect to get married, and there is no difference between the answers of boys and girls. What's the best age to get married? The teens told us 25.

And 98 percent of the teens say they want to have children. What's the ideal number of children to have? Over 80 percent say two or three.

The Birds and the Bees and the Rules

One other old standard remains: Parents aren't great at talking to their kids about sex. Teens, particularly boys, say they are most likely to learn about sex "pretty much on my own." Only 20 percent say they learned about sex from parents at home. But sex is one area where teens are showing a real shift in values from their parents—a change that could really affect the way we live in the years ahead.

A quarter of the USA's teenagers—a full 25 percent—say they don't consider it bad if an unmarried friend becomes pregnant; 42 percent consider it "not very shameful" while only 31 percent considered it very shameful for an unmarried woman to become pregnant.

Teens' attitudes become more liberal about this as they get older.

Now, these more liberal attitudes raise a serious concern. With most girls beginning sexual activity in their teens, the question of teen pregnancy and contraception looms large.

There is a positive response here, though. More than in previous generations, boys are accepting the responsibility for making sure girls don't get pregnant.

Among all teens, 61 percent say boys and girls share equal responsibility for contraception. And when we ask specifically if it's the boy's responsibility, boys are more likely than girls to say yes.

Only half of the USA's teens say their parents insist on meeting the people they date. Parents are twice as likely to want to meet their daughters' dates as their sons'.

And when it comes to what kids *don't* talk to their parents about, sex tops the list.

What don't you talk to the adults in your home about?	
Sex	20%
Personal relations	18
Things about school	10
Drugs, alcohol	8
Problems with friends	5

We can only hope we're getting a straight answer about the drugs and alcohol—that only 8 percent of teenagers are not talking to their parents about them—because the '80s became a very tough time to be a teenager and stay straight. Peer pressure to get involved with drugs or alcohol became intense. Remember here that we're talking about all teenagers, for most of whom even drinking beer is illegal. But when we asked teenagers about their friends we got these average results:

What percentage of your friends:	
Drink beer regularly?	44%
Drink alcohol regularly?	31
Use marijuana?	20
Use heroin and other drugs?	5

Don't take those statistics lightly. Kids are part of the Image Age, just like their parents; in some ways they're working even harder to live up to the expectations they sense around them. Girls, for example, just like their mothers, are only half as likely as boys to say they're satisfied with the way they look.

And *unlike* their parents, friends play a more significant role in teenagers' lives. With grownups, "family" was way ahead on this next question, but with teens, the top two are pretty close:

Which part of your life are you happy with?

My friendships	78%
My family	71
My health	69
My social life	61
My physical condition	57
The place I live	51
My school life	47
The way I look	38

Remember, that's a different kind of question than, "What's most important to you?" and elicits a different kind of answer—but it does point out the fertile ground for peer pressure, a potent force in the Image Age.

How Did You Do in School Today?

A few more points about parents and kids, including a few hopeful ones.

Guess what? Kids still read books. The average teenager has read over two books in the past month; a third have read four or more.

Guess what else? Parents could be doing more to encourage them. Only about one teenager in five says his parents limit his TV viewing. And how much good are those limits when parents do set them? Not much. Teenagers watch about three hours of TV every school day, whether parents limit their viewing or not.

It's not a lack of interest, because when we asked who's more concerned about the grades a teenager is getting in school, here was the answer:

My parents	58%
Me	38

(This changes abruptly, however, when teens reach 17—just when they're starting to think about getting ready for college or looking for a job.)

It seems pretty clear, though, that the more a parent is involved in the child's life, the better the child will do in school. A massive government survey of over 30,000 students showed a connection between good grades and parents who kept track of their children:

My Grades	Percent who say "parents almost always know where I am"
Mostly A's	88%
Mostly B's	81
Mostly C's	72
Mostly D's	61

What about homework? A third of all teens say they do less than an hour of work, and another 50 percent do less than two hours. Only 17 percent of all teens do more than two hours of homework—more girls than boys.

In fact, 39 percent of the boys spend less than an hour, compared with 26 percent of the girls.

Thirteen percent of the teens say their parents help them regularly with their homework. We didn't ask them, however, how much help they really were.

One Thing We All Agree on

Somehow, this doesn't surprise us here in the Image Age, but guess what area teenagers and their parents are *most* similar in? The desire for possessions—specifically the desire to own a car.

Teens: What's your most important possession?

Car	17%
Stereo	11
Collections, hobbies	7
Pet	7
Bicycle	6
Radio	6
Clothes	6

Grownups: What's your most important possession?

Car	22%
Television	17

House	7
Stereo	7
Pet	4
Sports equipment	4

The reports of the family's death have been greatly exaggerated. We still need the love of a family, we still desire the warmth of home and hearth, and, as we move into the '90s, we will see that as times get more confusing people will turn more and more toward the family for strength and support. It is the definition of the family that is changing—its structure, its shape, its many faces—but not its importance or the basic values that underlie it.

This is important to keep in mind as we move into the next chapter, on divorce.

CHAPTER SEVEN

Divorce

Washington state: A man's wife files for divorce. He uses a bulldozer to level their $85,000 home. Her response: "I guess he didn't want me to have anything."

Connecticut: A woman is in court waiting for divorce proceedings. Her husband pulls out a gun and shoots her. He is charged with murder. His response: "Now I can sleep at night."

London: A couple has decided to file for divorce. Her response: none. It seems the two haven't spoken a word to each other for 12 years, and even discussed their divorce by passing notes to each other.

For this is what divorce is about: Passion.

And, in the '80s, paradox.

On the one hand, our belief in the value of family life remains as strong as ever.

On the other hand, the divorce rate is growing to record levels. And the highly emotional release—an explosion of emotion, really—that results from divorce is important to focus on as we continue on our tour through the '80s and into the '90s.

The key to understanding divorce in the '80s is this: The strong emotional explosion is almost solely directed toward the individual's mate, not to the idea of marriage.

Before we talk about the emotions men and women feel as they go through a divorce, let's look at the facts.

Twenty-five years ago, 39 percent of all marriages ended in divorce. Today, about half of all new marriages will end in divorce.

What are the reasons for this? It's probably not coincidental that the divorce rate's climb comes as women are moving into the workplace in great numbers. The economic independence they've found has freed them to escape some bad marriages—and, as we noted in the last chapter, the stresses of a two-income family have probably ended some good ones.

Don't blame just women for this. Remember, a lot of the conflicts arise over men's confusion about their own sex roles and reluctance to get more involved with the responsibilities of the home (or give up some of their attention to work).

A government study found that people married after 1975 are significantly more likely than those married earlier to see their marriages end within five years.

Here's a scary fact: More than one out of four families with children is headed by a single parent. Some experts predict this will grow to one out of every three families by 1990.

As divorce becomes more common, it becomes more socially acceptable. A Philadelphia magazine even ran a "clip and save" article in one of its June editions: a bride's guide to divorce.

We're getting our divorces the old way (Nevada has the highest divorce rate in the nation, and Reno's still a favorite divorce spot). And we're finding some new ones—one famous divorce lawyer is producing a videocassette on everything you always wanted to know about divorce.

And finally, for reasons we won't even begin to guess at, marriages seem to fall apart faster in the West than in the East. For what it's worth:

Here are the states with the longest median durations of failed marriages:	
Massachusetts	9.2 years
Maryland	8.9
Pennsylvania	8.5
New York	8.4
Connecticut	8.3

And here are the states with the shortest median duration of failed marriages:	
Wyoming	5.0 years
Utah	5.1
Idaho	5.2
Kansas	5.3
Montana	5.3

So those are the numbers. Now let's look at what divorce is doing to us.

You Always Hurt the One You Love

To start off on an up note: Divorce can be a positive thing. Our interviews show that leaving a bad living situation can make people feel stronger and healthier emotionally. I had a problem in my life and I did something about it, they tell us.

Here's a survey result that seems to show the strong, lasting self-image that comes after a divorce, especially for women. Divorced women are twice as likely as married women, and significantly more likely than single women, and *much* more likely than divorced men, to rate themselves as "very independent."

Divorce, apparently, creates a feeling of independence, a feeling that is strengthened, not weakened, by later remarriage. In fact, women who get divorced and then remarry are the most independent of all.

Maybe that's because divorce is a hardening experience but marriage is a secure one. Going through a divorce and then remarrying leaves women with the strength of feeling independent—without the emotional insecurity of being alone.

Because being alone, people tell us, can be the most insecure experience of their lives.

The everyday burdens of life increase dramatically with divorce. There's more loneliness, and there are more things to be done alone. Physical problems, emotional problems, and financial problems all increase dramatically.

Results from several USA TODAY studies show graphically the impact of divorce. We analyzed responses to more than 5,000 interviews to learn how events such as marriage and divorce affect our well-being and outlook on life.

This research shows that divorced people are easily the least satisfied with their lives of any group in the nation, less satisfied than singles, less than even widows and widowers.

They are exactly half as likely as either married or single people to be happy with their jobs and financial security.

They are only 75 percent as likely to be happy with their health and 75 percent as satisfied with how their social lives are going.

Why is this? The main reason, people say, is a simple one: They have more burdens to shoulder and only half as many shoulders as before to carry the burden.

Half of all those divorced say divorce hurt them financially; even more so for divorcees with children. This is unfortunate since about half—men and women—also say divorce increases the work and problems they have to deal with at home. A large number say they have more emotional problems to handle, and, surprisingly, men are slightly more likely to have emotional problems than women are.

So is divorce better than staying in a marriage that isn't working? Well, most of those divorced say that despite the problems they have now, the emotional and physical and financial ones, they were worse off when they were married. They may not be happy, but most see it as a positive step.

A whopping 87 percent of divorced people say divorce is the best solution to a poor marriage. Slightly more women than men feel a divorce is the right answer: 83 percent of the men and 90 percent of the women.

While people are often more likely to say good things about actions they themselves have taken, those numbers are still pretty high. And perhaps more convincingly, eight out of 10 divorcees told us they're happier now that their marriages are over, including a phenomenal 93 percent of the women. Among men, 62 percent say they're happier now.

Still, 55 percent plan to marry again. More than half. As we noted in the last chapter, despite the pain and suffering of a bad marriage and a divorce, people are more likely than not to say they don't dislike marriage; they just couldn't live with that particular person anymore.

Young people are most likely to feel that way—79 percent of divorcees between 25 and 34, say, "That one didn't work but I want to try again."

And to end on another up note: We've got some evidence that divorce is not an incurable disease. Love is just as good the second time around. We compared people in second marriages to people in first marriages. Guess who says they're happier? It's a tie. And there's no difference between men and women.

Going It Alone

Divorce is a frightening time. Divorced people are lonelier than single people who've never been married. And the sad part is, we often go through this difficult period alone.

When we surveyed divorced people, more than half—56 percent—said they didn't get much help from neighbors, friends, or relatives. In many ways, men are less prepared than women for dealing with the turmoil and trauma of divorce. As we said earlier, women are better at forming support groups, networks to help them in trying times.

This is especially clear here: Among divorced people, men are twice as likely as women—*twice* as likely—to say they suffered through it alone.

Marriage, even a bad one, helps you learn to communicate with people of the opposite sex. Married people, even if they've been divorced before, are all more likely than single people to say they can communicate openly and easily with members of the opposite sex. But guess who's the exception here? Divorced men. They rate near the bottom when it comes to communicating with members of the opposite sex.

We asked divorced people in an extensive survey where they got practical help coping with life during their split—help with the groceries, help with the kids, help with the finances.

Then we asked who offered emotional support. In each case, men were more likely to stand alone.

Look at the figures on practical support. As you can see, parents are most likely to offer such help. Still, less than half say they got help from their parents. And again, men came out second best.

Here's where divorced people told us they got practical help during their divorce:

	Men	Women
Parents	42%	58%
Friends	34	55
Brothers and sisters	31	49
Other relatives	19	29
Neighbors	17	36

Men are also less likely to get emotional support from friends and relatives. Here's where people said they got emotional support during their divorce:

	Men	Women
Friends	52%	69%
Parents	48	71
Brothers and sisters	43	63
Other relatives	29	48

The Children of Divorce

Children are the nagging question mark overshadowing divorce. Should unhappy couples stay together for the sake of the children? Should they split? Who should raise the kids? These are difficult questions, and there are no easy answers.

A plethora of studies over the past half-decade have produced some frustratingly contradictory findings on how divorce affects boys versus girls, school performance, behavior, and ultimately, happiness.

All of these headlines appeared in newspapers within an 18-month period, all of them based on what generally pass for reputable studies:

"KIDS OF SINGLE PARENTS GET JUST AS MANY As"
and
"SCHOOLWORK SUFFERS AFTER A DIVORCE"

"DAUGHTERS SUFFER MOST AFTER DIVORCE"
and
"PRE-TEEN BOYS SUFFER MOST FROM A DIVORCE"

"KIDS AREN'T BROKEN BY THE BREAKUP"
and
"DIVORCE CLOUDS OUTLOOK FOR TEENS"

Some of these studies, which have received widespread coverage in the media, are based on less than 100 interviews. By contrast, our research is based on interviews with thousands of people across the nation. We'll look at some of these questions and tell you how most people feel, including men and women who have gone through a breakup.

Coping with the question of whether or not to stay in a marriage for the sake of the children—and whether that's better or worse for the kids themselves—is clearly beyond the scope of this book. If you're grappling with such questions yourself, we'd suggest putting down this book and getting in touch with a qualified professional counselor.

But we can tell you how adults across the USA feel about the toughest question in divorce—what about the children?—including the feelings of those who have faced that problem.

QUESTION: Should parents remain in an unhappy marriage for the sake of the children?

A vast majority of men and women say no. In fact, only 23 percent of all adults say children are an important reason for an unhappy couple to stay together. Among divorced people, those who have actually suffered the agony of breaking up, the results are even more clear-cut. Only 12 percent say children are reason enough to keep a marriage together.

QUESTION: Do the children of divorce have more problems to overcome?

Again, the results are clear, but not so encouraging. More than eight out of 10 adults—85 percent—say a breakup causes more problems for the children.

Now look at what divorcees think. And remember, we just noted that only 12 percent say you should keep the marriage together for the sake of the children.

Even those same divorcees admit that the divorce was hard on the kids. More than seven out of 10 said their own children suffered because of the breakup.

This is a crucial finding since a child born today has a 45 percent chance of going through a breakup of his parents.

QUESTION: Who's best able to raise the children, the mother or the father?

When we asked this question, about half of the people answering said they weren't sure or "it depends." Of those who picked a single parent, almost all said the child should live with the mother. Government statistics show that nine out of 10 children of divorce live with their mothers.

	Total	Men	Women
Mother	48%	46%	51%
Father	3	4	3
It depends	44	45	43
Not sure	5	5	3

So what does all that tell us? Well, the mother-versus-father choice seems easy—we've been saying throughout this book that neither men nor women have really budged from the traditional view of the woman as the main homemaker and child-rearer, no matter what her other responsibilities.

And what about the rest? People seem to be telling us that, as we all know, divorce is very, very hard on children. But despite that, people feel that if you want to break up with your spouse, you should do so anyway.

A generation ago we wouldn't have heard answers like that. The more selfless behavior of "staying together for the children" was much more prevalent.

This could be a horribly selfish trend. In trying to live up to the Image Age, people may be reaching for a level of self-satisfaction that really doesn't exist, and may be going after it no matter what the cost to those around them.

Or this could be a very healthy trend. People may be feeling that getting a child out of a bad environment, where mommy and daddy don't love each other, is better in the long run than trying to pretend that they're giving the child a "normal" home.

Which is it? That's not really a question for surveys. That's for you to decide.

The Lessons of Divorce

We've been talking about divorce in terms of "bad marriages," and perhaps that's as unfair as it is vague. People get divorced for all sorts of reasons—some healthy, some not so healthy.

What are the main reasons?

We asked a series of questions of both married and divorced people—questions about problems in relationships. With some of the problems we asked about, people who were divorced felt about the same amount of stress as people who weren't.

But with some other problems, the differences between married and divorced people were drastic. Does this mean that these are the causes of divorce? Maybe yes, maybe no. One thing is certain: People who divorced reported much more trouble in these areas. Clearly they are at least part of the breakup process. Let's take a look at those key areas in order.

No. 1: Emotional support.
People who became divorced were almost 40 percent more likely than married people to say their spouse didn't give them the emotional support and encouragement they crave. The difference between married and divorced people was more drastic here than for any of the other questions we asked.

No. 2: Common interests.
Divorcees were 32 percent more likely to cite stress in their marriages caused by a lack of common interests and goals. And in follow-up interviews they supported this, describing it as the fraying fabric of a divorce. You don't wake up one morning and decide you want a divorce, but rather you drift apart over a period of time—and the divergence of interests is one benchmark of the growing distance.

No. 3: Honesty.
We asked people if they could talk openly and honestly with their spouse (or ex-spouse) about their innermost feelings.

Divorced people were 25 percent more likely to say "no," that the lack of open and honest communication caused stress in their lives. Many felt they couldn't talk openly with their husband or wife without fear of being criticized or ridiculed.

No. 4: Feeling liked and appreciated.

Divorced people are 25 percent more likely to say that they don't feel liked and appreciated—and notice that we said "liked," not "loved." More than one in four divorcees said this was a problem in their marriage that led to serious marital stress—and this was especially true for women.

What about stress in marriage caused by financial problems? It comes in a distant fifth on our list, even though it's the thing that couples argue about most. Money is important, but secondary to building an open and honest relationship.

What came in next? Use of free time, followed by a surprise. Problems with sexual responsiveness ranked only seventh on our list of marital stress-builders. This agrees with our nationwide survey of almost 1,000 psychiatrists, who ranked sexual problems eighth on the list of reasons that people seek psychiatric help. Problems with marriage or intimate relationships ranked No. 1.

Divorce—Male Style

Most of the things we've been talking about affect men and women in similar ways, but there are a few things about divorce that affect men and women very differently.

One of the real scars for a divorced man is blame. Men tend to blame themselves for a divorce more than women do, which is doubly hard because, as we've noted several times, they don't have the support groups that women do to help ease this hidden hurt.

The male ego suffers as a result. Divorced men are only half as likely as married men to rate themselves as good husbands or fathers.

When divorced men remarry, some of this ego-deflation goes away. Remarried men are twice as likely as still-divorced guys to call themselves good at husbanding or fathering.

By comparison, divorced women are just as likely as married women to say they were excellent wives. And divorced women actually rate themselves higher as mothers than never-divorced women. Divorced men, in fact, are twice as likely as divorced women to downgrade their marital roles— they believe they did a poor job of being a married person and that's why the divorce happened.

On the flip side, men make up for that ego-flattening by feeling better about themselves in the workplace. Divorced men are significantly more likely than other men to consider themselves excellent employees: 75 percent rate themselves as top-notch workers, compared to 45 percent of single men and 54 percent of married men.

And when we ask about life satisfaction, divorced men rate the satisfaction of work equal to the satisfaction of being a father.

Clearly, divorced men take solace in other roles when their marriages fall apart.

Divorce—Female Style

Divorce changes women forever. They're tougher, more independent, more likely to feel they can stand on their own without the help of a man. Most of that doesn't disappear if and when they get married again.

One final, important note: Independence in no way distances divorced women from their children. Our surveys of women show that the importance of being a mother positively *soars* after the split: 65 percent of the divorced women call motherhood their most satisfying role, compared with 32 percent of the married women.

Think about that: divorced mothers are twice as likely as married mothers to feel that mothering is the most satisfying role in their life.

Maybe they're channeling the importance of being a wife into motherhood, or maybe something else is going on, but for all the problems people say that divorced children have, it's nice to note that mother loves them.

Now that we've looked at relationships in the home we'll turn our attention to another theater of life—the workplace.

CHAPTER EIGHT

Working in the '80s

You're at the office. The phone rings. It's your spouse, screaming over the receiver, telling you that you've just won a million bucks in the lottery.

Do you turn back to your desk and finish the work you were doing? Do you work the rest of the week?

It is a fantasy that everyone who toils for a daily wage has had at one time or another. Yes, you think. I'd keep working—for about two minutes. Just long enough to tell the boss what I think of him and his ancestry, kick the Xerox machine, and tell that creep in accounting who keeps sending my expense accounts back where to forward the rest of them.

There's no way you'd keep working.

Or is there?

We complain about work, we try to get out of it, we call in sick when we're not, we feel crummy when we walk in and crummier when we walk out. But more than anything else, we need it—not for the money, but for the soul. We are terrified at the thought of going through life without it.

We posed The Big Question to more than a thousand adults. Ask yourself: Would you continue to work if you didn't have to? If money weren't a problem, would you quit your job?

Only 16 percent of all adults—*not even two out of 10*—said they'd pack up their Rolodex and hit the road. About the same number said they'd keep working but switch jobs.

A full 50 percent of the working stiffs in the USA said they'd go on being working stiffs at the same job they're in right now.

Sure, that's easy to say. Maybe people *have* to say that to themselves to get through the day without shooting that guy who smokes a pipe in the next cubicle over—but what would people really do?

Well, a study by the Institute for Socio-Economic Studies recently published in USA TODAY looked at a lot of the people who've won a million dollars or more in a lottery; at the time there were about 1,200 of them. Guess what? Four out of 10 kept working at the same job they had when they won the big bucks. Only 16 percent retired altogether, just about what our research shows.

Think they're crazy? No crazier than you are. Almost eight out of 10 people say they're basically satisfied with their jobs.

And "basically satisfied" doesn't tell half the story. Because our connection to our job is more than that. Much more.

When we asked people if they enjoyed their work, three out of four said they do. There's an ethic of the workplace that seems to make it not-very-acceptable to go around wearing such feelings on your sleeve: "You Don't Have to Be Crazy to Work Here—But It Helps" has been a much more popular office plaque than "You Know, I Really Like It Here." But you know something? You really like it here.

Let's not lose the perspective. For married people, their role in life as husband or wife, as mother or father, is much more satisfying. Work places a distant third (of course, it's much higher among single people).

Take another look at the statistic we talked about a few chapters back when we asked people what was their most satisfying relationship:

Husband/wife	31%
Mother/father	30
Work	8

So remember as we go through this chapter that work does not occupy that special place in our hearts, does not form that cornerstone of our values, that the family does.

Work does something else, though. There is a magic to the workplace, created if nothing else by the familiarity of it. There is a closeness and an understanding, a language and an ethic, a history and a set of myths and fables and a structure— there is every element of an entire culture, an entire world.

You almost certainly spend more time at work than you spend at any other single activity in your life. You spend more time in the company of the person who sits next to you than you spend in the company of your spouse, your children, or even your television.

Think about it: 68 percent of us spend more than nine hours each day at work (including getting there and getting home). The median for all workers is about nine hours and 15 minutes.

That means, of course, that some people out there are working a lot of overtime. Who are they? By age, it's baby boomers who work the most overtime; by profession, it's salespeople, managers, and professionals.

Here's who works overtime:

Age	Percent working overtime
16-19	18%
20-24	26
25-44	34
45-64	31
65 and up	27

So if you work those nine hours, and add another eight hours for sleep (if you're lucky), what does that leave you?

Seven hours. Seven hours for reading, relaxing, taking a bath, watching TV (and you know *that's* eating up a lot of time), cleaning the house, calling your mother, helping your kids with the homework, making love, eating, taking out the garbage, going dancing, learning French, or doing volunteer work at Children's Hospital.

And that's if you *don't* bring work home.

Remember, one out of three workers brings work home from the office regularly. More than one in five of all employed adults bring work home at least twice a week.

So of those seven spare hours, subtract the average two

hours and six minutes we spend on the work we bring home.

Power of the Workplace

So work, for those of us who work, becomes an incredibly potent force—for good or evil, for change or stagnation, for creating a great sense of self-worth and love of life or creating a great sense of hopelessness and helplessness.

Through computer analysis of thousands of interviews, we found that working at a job you don't enjoy can have a terribly negative effect on your life, worse than having a serious illness, worse than not having enough time to do the things you want, worse than taking a pay cut.

Think about that one for a second. If your boss offered you a pay cut, but assured you that you'd enjoy your job more, would you take it? Probably not. But which hurts you worse, causes the most stress and anxiety? Not enjoying the job, by far.

The importance of the workplace to the psyche can't be stressed enough. We want to succeed there, we want to be needed there, we want to be appreciated there, we want to be loved there. Only one in 10 of us say we have a serious problem with our job—but about half of us vow to work harder.

We asked people a pretty straight question about the coming year: what they hope will happen in their immediate family. Here are the results:

What do you hope will happen in the next year?	
I get a promotion	68%
Spouse gets a promotion	64
I change jobs	31
Move	25
A marriage in the family	24
Spouse will change jobs	21
Will have a child	11
I will get divorced	1

Note well: The top three goals all deal with work.

By the way, let's stop here and explode one more little myth. If you could do anything in the world, *anything*, what would you do? You want to play centerfield for the New York Yankees? You want to be the lead singer for the Rolling Stones? Or you want to wear a suit and talk on the phone a lot?

Which would you rather be? Pick one:	
A rock star	( )
A professional athlete	( )
A business tycoon	( )

We posed that question to grownups—and believe it or not, if you're like most of us you chose to be a business tycoon.

That's what more than 60 percent of all adults chose, including 65 percent of the women.

Professional athletes ran a distant second at 24 percent; only 9 percent wanted to be a rock star.

The Next Workers

Now, if you think *you're* a workaholic, wait 'til you see what the next generation has in store. They're so ready to work at a straight, respectable, high-paying job it'll make your head spin.

We've mentioned before that 86 percent of all teens, including eight out of 10 girls, expect to be working full time by the time they reach age 30. Guess what they expect to be doing?

Don't look for any public-service careers at the top of the job wish-list for today's teens. They're not looking to save the world; their idea of saving appears to be a much more traditional one. We'll see in a future chapter that college students feel pretty much the same way.

The No. 1 career goal for today's teen-ager: computer science. No. 2: business. The next three: three more high-ticket slots—lawyer, doctor, engineer. This comes through even stronger when we look just at college students, which we will a few chapters from now.

We also asked teenagers to imagine themselves in a variety of positions—from becoming their own boss to president of the United States. Here's what they have in mind.

Teenagers: Can you imagine yourself:	
	Percent saying "Yes"
Being in a position where people work for you	91%
Making a great deal of money	89
Owning your own business	72
Meeting the president of the United States	28
Becoming president of the United States	6

Thank God It's Friday

All of this positive talk about work is making you a little uncomfortable, isn't it? Of course it is. It just doesn't make sense, does it? There must be something wrong with the statistics, mustn't there? If everybody's so damn crazy about jobs, how come nobody's smiling on the subway in the morning?

Maybe it's because the things that make work so important to us are deeper, less obvious to us on a day-to-day basis. There is no question, from looking at the survey results, that what happens to us from nine to five shapes our sense of self. But that psychological need isn't something that pops up in our minds when the alarm clock rings. Nobody wakes up saying "Oh, boy, it's a work day! Time to get up and feel like a useful member of society!"

Nevertheless, like it or not, an overwhelming number of workers derive a great deal of their sense of worth from what they do day-to-day. Why do all those lottery winners stay at their jobs? Why have so many women fought so long to be part of that rat race? Quite simply because a job—no matter what the job—helps people define who they are, and makes them feel like a part of something.

Now, that's all on a deeper level, a larger scale than we normally relate to work on. Day in and day out, there are things about the office that we absolutely, positively, totally, thoroughly, *hate*.

Let's start with Monday, the most maligned day of the week. Nobody who wants to stay on speaking terms with co-workers comes to the office in a cheery mood on Monday. It seems just deadly.

Guess what? It is.

A long-term study by the *Journal of American Insurance* showed that half of all executives who died at work died on Monday. And, of those who died just of heart attacks, 75 percent died on a Monday.

OK, what else do we hate about work? we asked. Here are your answers.

What upsets you most about where you work?	
Pay	11%
Lazy fellow employees	11
Poor management	11
Inefficiency	10
Lack of recognition	10
Office politics	9
Management lacks consideration	8
Job pressure	7
Attitudes of co-workers	6
Lack of opportunity	6
Other	11

Nothing really stands out here—lousy pay, lazy co-workers, crummy bosses all drive us nuts. Maybe our surveys just never hit on the thing that we really hate about the office—or maybe there is no one thing. Maybe it's just the compilation of things that are out of our control—money, other people, our bosses—that drives us up the wall.

It is interesting that when people finally get fed up enough to leave, the reason for leaving suddenly becomes clear. They want to move up and make more money. Two sometimes-conflicting desires—a more secure job and a more challenging one—were the runners-up; but getting ahead stood out.

Why people change jobs	
For better advancement opportunities	60%
To make more money	57
For better job security	38
For a more challenging job	36
To move to a better part of the country	15

| Spouse changed jobs | 13 |
| Transferred by my boss | 9 |

Remember, though—it may be clear why people take a new job, but it's not so clear why they didn't like the old one. And while we can't be sure, we'd bet that the frustrations at the new job aren't much different from the hassles at the job that was left behind.

Work and Real Life

OK, so that's the workplace. We love to hate it and we hate to admit that we love it.

But what is it doing to us?

First let's look at its effect on our personal relationships.

It's fascinating because it runs so contrary to what we have come to believe, but when both partners in a couple work, their relationship actually improves.

According to our surveys, couples in which both the man and woman work say they are less likely to argue about job pressures and demands. As we saw earlier, they are more satisfied with their home lives than in the "traditional" family where the wife stays home.

This isn't so strange, though, when you listen to what people told us in follow-up interviews. Some of the reasons are simpler than you'd think: A lot of people in two-worker couples say they simply don't have *time* to fight—that because the time they have to spend together is so precious, they very consciously protect against trivial fights, very deliberately avoid spending too much time bitching about work or talking shop at all. One working woman in San Francisco summed it up nicely: "By the end of the day," she told us, "we're simply too tired to fight."

We mentioned earlier that men say working women are better able to understand the pressures they're under, and that understanding—which goes both ways—helps the relationship. They also benefit in other ways. Compared to couples in which only one person works, working couples are:

■ 13 percent more likely to say they have more control over their lives.

- 45 percent more likely to say life is getting easier.
- 11 percent *less* likely to say life is getting harder.

There is, of course, a more practical reason that working couples seem to be having a little easier time with their relationship.

Money.

More than ever before, two income families are better off financially then one-income households. At the close of the 1970s, two-income families made 45 percent more than families in which only one mate worked. By 1984, that figure had risen to 56 percent.

Four out of five people who say they are satisfied with their jobs and finances also say they're happy with their lives. And 54 percent say they have a great deal of control over their lives, higher than the national average.

Money makes things happen. It also helps free us from the minor irritations of life. Remember all the conflict over household chores we talked about? Well, two-income couples are much more likely than anyone else to hire someone to do minor chores like vacuuming, laundry, and cleaning.

On the Road Again

The image of the mobile corporate executive may remain, but the fact is fading quickly. The lure of promotion is losing its attractiveness. The glamour of travel is fading quickly. Remember, we said earlier that work is the third most important thing in our lives, but far behind our mate and children.

We asked recently if people would take a better job if it meant moving from their present community. Here are the results:

Yes	33%
No	53
Depends on the job	12
Not sure	2

Remember that men are much more likely than women to move for a job. But among married people overall, two out of three say they would not move, while single people were pretty evenly split between moving and staying put.

People give us several reasons for moving becoming more unpopular—a fact that will probably continue to be a problem for companies in the immediate future and beyond.

For one thing, moving is expensive. Even with the generous relocation benefits many corporations offer, a major move usually costs us money and we need a big salary hike to justify the expense.

Another consideration, and one that will be harder for companies to solve, involves the growing number of two-career families. It's hard to ask your mate to give up his or her career so you can get a promotion. This is a problem that will grow as the number of two-income households soars. Firms are going to have to offer new types of benefits, including job-search help for spouses, to encourage transfers among their most promising workers.

Work and Kids

Thousands of articles have been written about "latchkey children," the kinds of articles that can make working parents feel terribly guilty.

And it's true that children in families where mom and dad work have some very special problems that need careful tending.

But take heart: A variety of studies have concluded that your children don't necessarily suffer because both parents work.

In fact, one study conducted by the National Assessment of Educational Progress concluded that the children of working mothers actually read better than their classmates whose mothers stay home.

Working parents seem to instinctively understand this: There isn't as much guilt out there as one might expect.

We went to homes where both parents work. We asked them to compare their kids to children in homes where only one parent works.

Working parents felt their children were:	
Better off	23%
As well off	52
Not as well off	19

So three out of four working parents feel their children are at least as well off as their more traditional counterparts. That's good news, since more than half of all new moms who worked before childbirth return to work within a year, a rate 25 percent higher than a decade ago.

The Working Woman, Continued

The movement of women into the labor force has had a profound impact on our way of life and the way we raise our children. And although there are about 6 million wives making more money than their husbands, we said earlier that women make only about 64 cents for each dollar a male makes. Women remain concentrated in the traditionally female fields. In 1982, 99 percent of all secretaries, 96 percent of nurses, and 82 percent of all elementary teachers were women. Women are making inroads, however, as this study by the Conference Board, a New York-based economic research group, shows:

Percent of women as a total of each occupation:

	1960	1982
Accountants	16%	39%
Lawyers/judges	3	14
Doctors/dentists	7	14
Nurses	98	92
Bus drivers	10	47
Bank officers	12	38

Work and the Computer

Thanks largely to computers, workers will have less tedious work to do than in years past. They will be freer to do more creative work. This will lead to more job satisfaction.

These predictions fly in the face of much speculation that the high-tech workplace will be more impersonal, more sterile, a less satisfying place to work.

Almost 31 million adults use a computer at work, and for the vast majority of us, the experience has been good. In fact, a staggering 91 percent of all people who use a computer at work tell us they are happy with the way computers have changed their work lives. And 54 percent of them are very happy with their computers. Remember, we're not talking just about people involved in computer programming or computer science. We're talking about all employees, from business executives to clerks.

This will grow. Three out of four of all adults tell us it's *very* important for people to learn how to use computers.

About 8 million people who use computers at work also have them at home. And those people are much more likely than others to work at home; 44 percent take work home regularly—51 percent of the men and 32 percent of the women.

Discrimination

While the '60s defined a goal for a generation—the elimination of discrimination—the '80s have seen a raging debate over how to achieve that goal. Cries for affirmative action were answered with echoes of reverse discrimination. Hiring goals were challenged, anti-segregation programs were summarily dumped.

Again, it's not within the scope of this book to take up the argument, but we do want to report what the people in the USA tell us they feel is happening.

We recently did a survey with an "oversample," an unusually large number of interviews, with black adults. Our goal: to compare attitudes between whites and blacks, men and women toward their experiences in work and toward equal opportunity.

We asked over 1,500 adults if there was a specific instance over the past year when they felt discriminated against on the job because of race.

Here's who said yes, they've felt discriminated against:	
White	8%
Black	23
Hispanic	21

Think about that for a second: More than one out of five black and Hispanic workers say they've experienced job discrimination over the past year.

Now, we can't prove whether this discrimination actually exists or not. The key point here is that the perception of discrimination is still strong.

The perception of discrimination among women is almost as great. About 17 percent of all women feel they've suffered from sex discrimination in the workplace within the last year. (By comparison, less than half as many men felt that way.)

To what degree are equal opportunity programs cutting into that perceived or actual discrimination?

Among blacks, 16 percent say they have received a job or educational opportunity through an equal opportunity program; Among women, 7 percent say they got a job opportunity at least partially thanks to equal opportunity.

One way more workers, and particularly women, are battling discrimination—and gaining independence—is by starting their own firms. The number of self-employed people in the USA has grown 24 percent over the last 10 years.

As we'll see in the next chapter, Horatio Alger is alive and well.

Who They Are

There's plenty of sweat, plenty of hard work, and lots of stick-to-itiveness in the stories of these people who started, in most cases, with just a few thousand dollars and built it into millions.

Their average age is now 43. The average age when they started out on their own was only 34.

Few were rich when they set out. Several even started their businesses with cash advances borrowed from their credit cards. Few were genuises or distinguished scholars in school. A third were in the top third of their class, but 42 percent said they were in the middle or below.

What did they excel in at high school? About 30 percent excelled in varsity sports; 20 percent stood out in club and church activities; 15 percent in music and art. But the answer at the top of the list surprised and delighted us: More than anything else, the Inc. 500 founders said they were best at getting into trouble.

The car they are most likely to own now is a Mercedes— followed pretty closely by a Chevrolet. Golf, skiing, tennis, and boating are their top hobbies (though three like to play with model trains, two love crossword puzzles, and one is into ballooning); 57 percent read the *Wall Street Journal*, 26 percent read USA TODAY, 12 percent read the *New York Times*.

They were fired or lost their jobs more frequently than the average adult. A full third of these company founders have been fired from a job at some time during their career or replaced by someone else. Yet few say problems at their pre-vious job were what caused them to strike out on their own.

They worry about the nation, and they're enamored of the work ethic. As you might expect, 51 percent consider them-selves conservatives and another 39 percent say they're con-servative on many issues. Eighty percent say they're most likely to support Republican candidates and 82 percent voted for Ronald Reagan.

There are some other interesting, less obvious common elements among these uncommon people. Some go back to their childhoods.

About half were either the oldest or only child in their

households. Most were from middle-class backgrounds: 79 percent said they hailed from the working class or middle class, while only 2 percent said their parents were wealthy.

And while 72 percent had at least a college degree (11 percent said they never went beyond 12th grade), 57 percent said their fathers never went beyond high school.

Perhaps most fascinating: They are far more likely than the average worker to be sons or daughters of people who worked for themselves; 46 percent say that at some point their parents started their own business and 51 percent say that at some point their parents ran their own business.

It isn't that entrepreneurism is something that runs in the blood. In in-depth interviews they tell us that seeing someone else start his own business or run his own company gave them the confidence that they, too, could be independent.

"You must *think* you can do it," said one founder. "You must have ambition and be self-motivated, with an ego, willing to take falls and pick youself back up and start over again. It takes a lot of nerve to start out on your own, and a lot to continue."

Why People Take the Risks

For all these people, success at business has been a dream come true. Almost nine out of 10 members of the Inc. 500 tell us that the success of their business has allowed them to accumulate more wealth than they ever would have been able to while working for someone else. That's certainly understandable, since their average net worth is just under $5 million.

So that's the motivation, right? It certainly seems like enough motivation for the average person.

But it's not. The desire for money is not the main reason these people say they took the risk of starting their own business. It's not even second on their list. Or third. Or fourth.

When we asked the Inc. 500 entrepreneurs what drove them to take the leap, they said it was the desire for personal satisfaction, for independence, for control over their own lives.

We asked them on our survey to list the main reasons they went into business for themselves. Here is what they said:

What are the main reasons you went into business for yourself?

Desire to control my life	89%
Desire to be my own boss	81
Wanted to prove I could do it	66
Desire to create something new	60
To make money and acquire wealth	55
Frustration of dealing with the bureaucracy of a large company	47
Trouble getting ideas forwarded	32
Wasn't being rewarded in previous job	31
Felt I didn't fit into a larger organization	22
Felt I wasn't advancing in my previous job	18

Notice also how different their responses were from those of the general public who, as we saw in the last chapter, listed the top reason for leaving their job as advancement opportunities and money—with nothing else coming close.

For the Inc. 500, the top four reasons all dealt with a variety of responses related to personal independence. Making money ranked only fifth on the list.

There's something else very important buried in these findings. Despite the fact that they get fired more often than usual, these people were't all that unhappy in their previous jobs. Frustration with their firms, lack of reward, and lack of advancement all placed at the bottom of the list.

In all likelihood, these successful entrepreneurs would have been successful even if they had stayed in their old jobs. The move had less to do with what they were leaving behind than what they were headed for.

Most left not because of problems with their previous employers, but because of a need within themselves, a need, as we've seen, that's growing in the '80s. And the number of new businesses cropping up indicates that people in the USA are acting on that need.

There were 600,000 new businesses started in 1985, the most in history.

That's good for the nation. The number of people who work for themselves grew almost 6 percent during the early '80s, compared with growth of just over 1 percent in the number of wage and salary workers, according to government statistics. These companies added twice as many jobs as the large national corporations did. And that doesn't count the "secondary" jobs that are created. These new firms engage in the new trend of "farming out" lots of tasks, such as public relations and travel planning, creating jobs in those industries too.

But our focus here is more on what this all means for the individual entrepreneur—who, by the way, is still overwhelmingly likely to be a male, but maybe not for very much longer.

While only about 4 percent of the Inc. 500 are women, government statistics show that women are going into business for themselves at a rate five times faster then men. Women have one added incentive that men don't: A great way to eliminate job discrimination is to be the boss.

Getting Started

Few of us were born rich, or excelled in school, or even had parents who went into business for themselves. But that doesn't mean we can't be very successful in business. In fact, a look at the Inc. 500 shows that just about anyone with the courage and the determination can be successful. Remember, these are among the most successful, most affluent people in the USA. Yet few had big bucks to risk when they started out.

The vast majority worked for another company before they started out, with a fairly even split between large corporations and small firms. This gave them badly needed experience, but also a chance to plan and save money to go out on their own.

Almost three-quarters of the Inc. 500 for 1985 and 1986 said that savings accounted for a substantial portion of the money they needed to start their companies.

They started with an average of $33,800; not an insignificant amount but certainly not out of reach for many of us. You would save that much in just over eight years by putting aside $50 a week, compounded by interest.

Many of the Inc. 500 scrounged their money up from as many as three or four different sources. And many were quite creative about doing it.

To find out how they got started, we asked the founders of these firms where they got the money to set up their companies:

Where they got the money	
Personal savings	71%
Bank loans	31
Other family members	20
Mortgaged property	17
Friends	11

It's worth adding here that only 4 percent say they got help from state and federal programs such as the Small Business Administration. And only 2 percent got any cash from "venture capitalists"—people who loan money to new firms solely to make money—although they've taken on mythic proportions from all that's beeen written about them in the popular press.

What you don't read much about are the ingenious ways you can get cash when you've made the decision to take the plunge and start out on your own.

Consider these actual cases from the Inc. 500:

■ Five used the cash value of insurance policies to help set themselves up in business.

■ One entrepreneur used royalties he received from writing a book; one used his discharge money from the U.S. Air Force.

■ Several used tax refunds to help strike out on their own.

■ One used severance pay from a previous job.

■ Four founders of Inc. 500 companies used cash advances from credit cards to fund themselves in getting started.

They started with an average of two partners, although many tell us now that if they had it to do over again, they'd avoid having partners at all costs.

And for those of you who've started your own business already and are wondering why you did such a crazy thing, take solace in this: Most of our founders had lots of trouble when they started out.

"Be prepared to work harder and longer than you ever

thought possible," advises one businessman.

"I found that my most essential attribute has been perseverance," said another. "Leadership skills, which I've had to develop, and creativity were also important, but perseverance has been essential."

And with good reason. Sixty percent of the Inc. 500 had to take a pay cut when they started their companies. And more than two out of three, 68 percent, said they had to reduce their standard of living to help the firm survive. And 79 percent said they missed paychecks or took no salary on occasion when they were getting the company started.

But there are two questions that really show what kinds of pressure they were under:

What would have happened if your business failed?

Eight out of 10 say they would have been personally wiped out or at least severely damaged financially. That's one thing that's so appealing about this group, and makes them so intriguing in light of the great desire people feel to take control of their own lives in the '80s.

They emerge as people who, for the most part, started like anyone else. Each was a worker in a job who decided to take a chance. But they also emerge as people who do what most only dream of having the courage to do: leaving a comfortable job to put their futures on the line.

There is also a cost of a more personal nature. More than a third of those who were married told us the pressure and stress of starting their company damaged their relationship with their spouse; 51 percent said they had to dramatically reduce the amount of time they spent with their family, and 64 percent said they had to cut out recreation and other activities that they enjoyed.

Was it worth it?

This brought the highest unanimity of any single question on the entire survey. Ninety-five percent said they would do it all over again. They would quit their job and start their own companies despite the financial risk, despite the sacrifice.

Now remember that these are mostly men, and we've already learned that men in the '80s *say* their families are most important but *act* as though they're willing to put the job ahead of everything else. So that may be part of the reason. But there's another reason these entrepreneurs say with such assurance that they made the right move despite the losses in their personal life. And it isn't money. They say that what they gained is more important than money. What they gained is freedom.

That, in fact, is the prescription for success that the Inc. 500 founder left us with. As one put it succinctly, here's what you have to do: "Hate working for somebody else. Believe you can do the job better and be willing to work hard."

There's also a lesson in this for other companies, large and small. The old rules no longer apply when you want to attract and keep the best people—the ones you look for to troubleshoot problems and launch new products. They're no longer satisfied going through life taking orders from the home office.

More firms will have to consider creating "individual centers" for innovation and independence within their large bureaucracies if they are to keep their best people. This must be an environment where executives can stretch, create, make mistakes, and learn from them, and in the process enrich their own lives and their companies' profits.

These, we predict, will be the "air pockets" of the '90s— little protected enclaves within big companies that can act independently. They'll have the freedom to get to know their customers better than the big corporation does; they'll be able to respond more quickly to changes in marketing and technology; they won't have to go too far up the bureaucracy to get the OK for an idea, and therefore will be able to focus on the creativity and power of their people. They'll be little speedboats buzzing around the huge, slow-steering ocean liner of bureaucracy.

Making a Go of It

If there's one thing that almost every entrepreneur stressed in our survey and in personal interviews later, it's that one of the biggest factors to success is the "sweat factor." Take the number of hours you think you're going to work and multiply by two.

The hours are long. Inc. 500 leaders told us that while starting out they spent an average of 64 hours a week on the job.
That's from about eight in the morning until nine at night,
five days a week.

Even now, an average of nine years and millions of dollars
later, a 54-hour workweek—almost 11 hours a day—is standard. That's a funny concept of freedom, but freedom is what
they call it, and long hours is what it takes.

"If you want to make it highly successful, it will take far
more time, effort, and personal toil than you can ever imagine," says one chief executive officer who has made it big. "All
of your thoughts, both waking and sleeping, are channeled to
the success of the business. Everything else takes a back seat.
If you are not prepared to make this commitment, you will
either fail or have only moderate success."

And contrary to what you may have heard or read, people
who run their own businesses don't have less job stress than
the rest of us. Now, however, they're worried about the competition rather than the boss.

They're no more likely to have their marriages end in
divorce than are any of the rest of us, even though they admit
that starting their businesses caused a great deal of stress
with their mates. One reason, a CEO and company founder
told us: "You must have the total, unqualified support of your
family [because] you must be prepared to eat, sleep, and drink
your business."

One out of five said they needed their spouse's income to
survive during the tough years while their business was starting; 38 percent said their wives have worked in the business;
and 34 percent said their wives still do.

Here's what they said are their major sources of stress:	
Business finances	56%
Time commitments	46
Pressure to succeed	43
Business competition	39
Employees	21
Relationship with spouse	20
Relationship with children	14

Personal finance	13
Health	12
Relationship with other family members	5

Learning to Manage

There was one thing that surprised many of these highly successful executives: Not everyone wants, or is willing, to work as hard as they are. They had to learn how to deal with these people and others on the job.

In fact, for the most part, these people did not start out as good managers. It's ironic that what many had to struggle with were success and learning to manage.

It's just one of the problems they had to deal with once their business finally took off. We'll discuss this more later, but it's worth noting here that being a manager isn't something that these people found came naturally to them. Remember, it was a need for independence that led them to the decision to set out on their own, not any sense that they'd be a good boss.

And sometimes, quite candidly, they aren't. The qualities that build a good company aren't always the ones that keep it going.

A number of CEOs took time out to expound on this very point. When we asked them what advice they'd give someone in their position, here's what they had to say:

1. Develop a good plan with written objectives and follow it.

2. Hire good people and delegate to them.

3. Don't assume that everyone is motived by what motivates you.

4. Don't be afraid to seek outside advice. Put together an outside board of advisers, or even a board or directors. Everyone needs a boss to report to, even you.

5. Have a backup in mind for every key person in the place, including yourself.

That's the hardest to accept for people who started a business from scratch. Exactly half of the Inc. 500 told us that there's no one in the company who can replace them on a day-to-day basis. Clearly, this is an invitation to disaster.

Inside the Inc. 500

Let's kill another myth. Most entrepreneurs aren't looking to get rich quick and then cash out.

While 56 percent of executives in the Inc. 500 have been approached by someone wanting to take their firms public (in other words, sell stock to the general public), only 19 percent say they want that to happen; 25 percent say the chances are fifty-fifty, while 56 percent say they do not want to take the chance of losing control of their company.

Much the same goes for selling their company; 76 percent say they've been approached by someone wanting to buy their firm but only 20 percent say they definitely want to sell; 36 percent would at least consider selling while 43 percent give a flat-out no.

These people are building a business, an extension of themselves. They're not looking to get rich quick.

This comes through in another way: While almost half plan to delegate more responsibilities to other people, only 14 percent say they plan to turn over day-to-day responsibilities to someone else.

There is, however, another reason: children. Seventeen percent say they have sons involved in their business, and 10 percent say daughters are involved. And 68 percent say they would want their kids to go into their business. When we asked this question of people in other lines of work, we got a very different sort of answer; only 30 percent of doctors, for example, said they want their children to follow in their footsteps.

A few other interesting traits about the Inc. 500 entrepreneurs: 23 percent smoke cigarettes or cigars, less than the national average of 32 percent. They eat lunch at their desk an average of twice a week. They go out to lunch on business about twice a week. And the fifth day, they don't eat lunch at all.

They are more informal than executives in major public industries: 49 percent wear formal business clothes, 32 percent say they wear casual clothes, and 19 percent—about one in five—wear casual attire such as blue jeans.

And to answer the burning question of our time: No, having a neat desk isn't a sign of success. Only 22 percent of our successful entrepreneurs describe their desks as neat and orderly. About 60 percent say their desks are scattered with papers, while 19 percent say their desks are very messy.

Lessons from the Inc. 500

So there you have a quick glimpse inside the Inc. 500—people who've done what many of us say we want to do in the '80s: people who've taken control of their own lives.

While we had this unique chance to pick the brains of the chiefs of the fastest-moving companies in the USA, we asked them for a bit of advice: What can our readers learn from them? What did they wish they knew before striking out on their own? What advice would they pass on to someone considering following in their footsteps?

In other words, could I do this? And how?

Some of the advice was conflicting. One Inc. company founder advised, "Never deal with banks," while another suggested, "Develop a good working relationship with your banker."

One founder said, "Burn your bridges; then you *have* to succeed." Another advised: "Don't burn your bridges behind you."

Sorting through all that, we put together the most often-mentioned kinds of advice to form a practical primer on business in the 1980s. In the next few pages, we'll tell you what the founders of the 500 fastest-growing businesses in the USA have to say about how to become No. 501.

We start with our Top Ten—the best advice from some of the most successful people in the USA.

The top ten tips

1. Business ought to be fun.

2. Business is built by will. If you don't have the will, go to work for someone else.

3. People, people, people. Go for the best.

4. If you can't sell your own product, forget starting a business.

5. Pay constant attention to cash flow. A lot of companies have gone out of business by being too successful.

6. Don't grow faster than your ability to manage the com-

pany. This is especially true when it comes to controlling costs.

7. After you get going, find people smarter in specific areas than you are. Hire them and make them responsible.

8. Everything costs more than you think it will cost. Everything takes longer. There are no bargains at the success counter.

9. In every crisis there is opportunity.

10. Persistence is all that is required.

Getting started

If you're tired of working for someone else, have a good idea and lots of energy, you can still get rich in the USA by going into business for yourself. But do your homework. Make sure you have enough capital to get through the first year. And discuss it with your family first. Here are some suggestions from the Inc. 500 founders on getting started.

1. *Do it!* Don't wait, because youth is important for energy. And when you're young, you can't fail because you can always start over again.

2. There comes a time when you have to take a gamble and give up the security of working for someone else. It is much easier if your wife or husband agrees with your decision.

3. Work for a large company and a small company to get experience. That way, you let someone else pay for your mistakes.

4. Don't think too much before you go out on your own. You might not do it and later will regret not having tried it.

5. Other businessmen will help you. They understand your difficult situation.

6. Ignore people who say your projections are too optimistic. They're right, but if you listen to them you'll never get started.

7. Start up in an area where workers are available.

8. Do extensive research prior to start-up. You'll need to know your market and your customers.

9. Formula for failure: Try 32 times.
Formula for success: Try 33 times.

10. Do not be undercapitalized. Triple your initial budget estimate for capitalization and start-up costs.

11. The most important step in starting a new business is to investigate your potential marketplace, discover a void in either products or services in that area, then rigorously establish your position within that void. Have a desire to work, work, work.

Finally, one additional comment seems to sum things up:

12. Set high goals and be willing to make the commitment—not just a contribution. Said one founder, "I remind myself of this each morning I have bacon and eggs for breakfast, that the chicken made a contribution, but that the pig made a commitment."

Planning your strategy

Develop a plan but be flexible. Situations change and you have to be flexible enough to take advantage of them. Identify your market niche and update your strategy regularly.

1. Plan your work, preferably in writing, and then work your plan.

2. Always have a backup strategy for dealing with situations involving loss of critical resources. What would you do if a major supplier or a major customer went out of business?

3. Your plan has to be flexible, to meet changing market situations. Nothing is carved in stone.

4. Seek advice and discuss your moves carefully. But be able to make bold moves when necessary.

5. Continue to develop plans and concepts for your company even after the business takes off.

6. In most cases, the things that happen to your business are never as good or as bad as they seem at the time.

7. Don't lose sight of your long-term goals in the maze of daily decision-making.

8. Don't listen to what the other person's deal is and then try to meet it. You tell them what yours is and that they can take it or leave it.

9. Don't try to make money; try to fill a need. The money will follow.

10. Don't try to be everything to everyone. Define your market, be the best, charge a fair price to make a profit.

11. Have a business plan. "I didn't," said one founder— "that's why it took me so long to get here."

12. Four prerequisites for success: a sound business plan,

good marketing, a unique product, and smart employees.

Managing your business
Concentrate on profits, not revenue. Manage for productivity and do not grow faster than you can manage—the people or the cash. Create opportunities for your employees and delegate responsibilities. It's vital to build a solid management team.

1. Control your growth, watch your costs, and delegate wherever you can.
2. Invest in areas you are completely knowledgeable in.
3. Profits must come first, before expenses.
4. The most important thing to the success of your business is sales—always.
5. Make sure expenses are always in line with sales. If they're not, act immediately to get them back in line.
6. Get involved with your community; eventually it all comes back to you.
7. Stick with it; it takes far longer than you would ever dream. Then when it finally starts to go, hand off day-to-day responsibility to managers more specifically qualified than yourself.
8. Recognize and accept your shortcomings, select the best talent and delegate to the extreme, as long as you retain veto power.
9. Learn from your mistakes but dwell on your victories.
10. Pay particular attention to cash flow. You can go broke by being too successful. Remember that when the cash flow is bad, you're the first person not to get a paycheck.
11. Keep a close eye on margins. Don't let revenue growth be your main goal. Profitability is really your ticket to staying in business.
12. Recruit a sound group of outside directors; you need to report to someone.
13. Raise money when you don't need it. It's a lot harder to get when you're in a jam.
14. Be aggressive from a marketing standpoint. Be financially conservative.
15. Always make ultraconservative projections and then reduce them by 30 percent.

16. Anyone can deal with failure; it's success that can kill you. Growth is exciting, stimulating, and dangerous.

17. Do not get involved in each deal; build an organization to handle deals. You need a solid management team that you can trust.

18. Keep growth as stable as possible.

19. When on a down cycle, don't wait too long to lay off employees, and bring expenses under control.

20. Stay on top of your accounts receivable.

21. Spend money when you have it with the same care you exercised when you didn't have it.

Managing yourself

Don't underestimate the amount of work starting your own business will take. But also, don't underestimate yourself. If you have a good idea and work hard, you can be successful.

1. Hard work is absolutely essential for success. There is no substitute whatsoever.

2. Be sure you know your limitations and either increase your capabilities, get good advice, or hire someone with the capabilities that you need.

3. Don't underestimate yourself or your product. Get involved yourself to create a market.

4. You probably know more about things than you think you do. Don't rely on attorneys and accountants to tell you about your product. It is "what you know ain't so" that can help or destroy you.

5. Time is a very precious commodity. You must learn to use it wisely.

6. Follow your common sense and never compromise on quality.

7. Work for other firms to gain experience in all areas of business.

8. Call your shots to the best of your ability and if you're wrong, admit it. Then work hard to correct your mistakes.

9. Base all your decisions on establishing a reputation of integrity. People like to do business with those they can trust.

10. Listen to your gut feelings and sometimes to your spouse.

11. First become organized yourself. Soon your company

will be organized also.

12. Spend time with family; they are your real treasure on earth. Force yourself to take time off—then enjoy it.

13. If you're not having fun, you're paying too high a price.

14. Forget the Big Shot Syndrome; be sincere and humble.

15. Remember that greed is the worst enemy of good judgment.

16. Always be yourself. Don't bullshit. People will react to honesty.

17. Be a risk-taker. Never give up. Work smarter. Get the best help you can find.

18. Be persistent and be patient and, most important, never give up.

19. Enjoy the ride; it's more important than the destination.

Managing your employees

1. People build a company, so take a personal interest in hiring people.

2. Hire the best people you can afford. It will pay dividends soon, and you can't afford less.

3. Have a backup for every key employee (including yourself).

4. The key to success is to motivate the employees. An incentive system that is substantial, fairly applied, includes stock, and allows employees to keep a running score will provide powerful motivation.

5. Learn when to hire and when to fire.

6. Be careful with commitments you make to employees hired early in the life of the company. The business is likely to outgrow them. Withdrawing the commitments may be traumatic and legally dangerous.

7. Don't expect or seek conformity in your people. Your job is to find the right drummer for each person in the march.

8. Be firm but fair with employees—and fire nonperformers early. Don't hesitate in terminating employees who are not performing.

9. Select key staff from people you trust and respect.

10. Identify your personal strengths and weaknesses and surround yourself with people (employees, advisers) who support you in the weak categories.

11. Don't hesitate to surround yourself with people who are smarter than you.

Beating the competition

1. Hit your competitors where they aren't. Develop a single area in which you can excel, and push it to the limit.

2. Public relations is extremely important. In today's world, perception is reality. Keep your company before the public.

3. Think hard about both your potential customers and competitors. Know your market better than anyone.

4. Know the industry you will be entering. Define your markets, have extensive information on your competition.

5. Talk to customers and employees all the time.

6. Undersell your competitors.

7. Never underestimate your competitors and always consider them to be a vital spur to your quest for success.

Learning as you go

A person starting his or her own business needs to be reasonably skilled in many areas of business, including marketing, employee relations, bookkeeping, finance, advertising, real estate and leases, and purchasing. But you don't have to be your firm's expert in each field. You can run a restaurant without knowing how to cook.

1. Learn to know and understand finances and accounting.

2. Continue to educate yourself even after your company starts taking off.

3. Knowing what you don't know is more important than what you do know.

4. You only learn from mistakes. Permit them to happen, but know you will learn from them.

5. A good knowledge of finance, marketing, sales, and distribution is absolutely necessary.

Taking a partner

Many founders tell us not to take a partner, if you can possibly help it. If you must, then be prepared.

1. If you can avoid it at all, don't take on partners, no matter how well you know them.

2. If partners are required for financial or "emotional" rea-

sons, choose very, very carefully. A divorce in a business is just as traumatic and expensive as a personal one.

3. Select partners that will contribute to the company and complement your own skills.

4. Know your partner better than you know your wife.

5. Who your partners and employees are will absolutely make you or break you. A bad partner is worse than no partner.

Serving the customer

1. Service to customers builds repeat sales. *Never* let your customers down.

2. Avoid extending credit on emotional bases. "Customers are perishable" is a valuable adage.

3. Sell service and back it up.

4. Keep your word!

5. Treat your customers as you would like to be treated.

6. Remember it's the customer who really signs your paycheck.

7. Service to the customer must be the primary goal of any company, and all who work there must understand that service—not money—is the goal.

8. Focus on your client's needs. Always work for his best interests.

9. Give your customers the best service you can possibly give them. In most cases, this is even more important than the price you are charging them.

The luck of the draw

1. Nothing beats being in the right place at the right time.

2. Luck comes to everyone at times. Be ready for it. Be satisfied with small gains.

3. Take a chance: Luck and being in the right place at the right time plus a commitment to quality and service are 90 percent of the success formula.

4. Go for the gold. Work hard. Make your own luck.

Well, there you go: the quickest guide to success you'll ever read. We'll leave the subject with three more points worth remembering, culled from the bosses of the Inc. 500:

- Your true security is in what you know and what you can do, not in working for a large organization. Take the risk!
- If you ever turn the corner, owning your own business is the best life in the world.
- In the USA, one is limited only by one's ability.

CHAPTER TEN

Aging in the '80s

George Burns is still having fun and making people laugh at age 90. After testifying in a dispute involving Groucho Marx's estate and Marx's companion Erin Fleming, Burns was asked if an 80-year-old man can find happiness with a 30-year-old woman. "No, not often," he said. "Only once or twice a night."

"A lot of old people are glad I'm around," Burns said in a USA TODAY interview. "It shows you don't have to retire. I think that's for the birds. What do you do when you retire? You sit around and look at your cuticles. Guy at 65 retires? He's still a kid."

Burns's spirit is testimony to the fact that growing old in the USA is not a sentence anymore, but a reward.

The images attached to old age—especially in the youth-oriented '60s and the yuppie-oriented '80s—have not been flattering ones. At best we imagined old age as a relief from the grind of having to get up early every morning. At worst we considered it a time of having no real reason to get up at all. About the best thing anyone had to say about old age is that it wasn't so bad, once you considered the alternative.

The loss of income, the loss of prestige, the loss of independence that come as people grow older colored our view of old people.

The Pepsi Generation has always been enamored of itself, of its youth, of its vitality; live fast, die young, and leave a good-looking corpse, said John Derek in *Knock on Any Door.* "Hope I die before I get old," screamed The Who in "My Generation."

But all of the focus we've placed on youth has neglected one simple fact.

Old people are happier than young people are.

Our surveys turned up some startling facts about old people.

They are more satisfied with their lives—how they live, what they do—than any other group in the USA. And despite the lack of respect we pay them, the increasing pressure to move them out of the workplace, the growing inability of society to figure out what to do with them—despite all that, the feeling of satisfaction they have seems to be growing every year.

The '90s may very well go down in history as the decade during which we finally learn that the elderly are really a national resource—and not just because they're such available baby sitters.

"The elderly" are properly defined as those "somewhat old, past middle age" (note that says nothing about one foot in the grave).

Why are they becoming so important?

First of all, there are more of them. By their very numbers they are forming a potent force that will become even more powerful in the years ahead. More than one in 10 of us are over 65. And that will grow to one in five in the next 45 years.

Second, their lifestyles are remarkably different from previous generations of old people. They're more active, happier, healthier, and wealthier; ready and willing to spend their money to maintain their independence and have fun (yes, believe it or not, old people do have fun).

There is no question that the elderly face some of the most serious problems in the USA. The rising cost of health care hurts them the most, as does the seeming inability of this country to take care of its hungry and homeless. They are the most likely to lose a job, a loved one, a way of life.

We don't wish to turn away any of the much-needed attention being paid to those problems. For those elderly who need
our help, it is a national disgrace that we can't return more of
what they've put into this country. What we do wish to do in
this chapter is blow away the myth that the elderly are, as a
group, useless, inactive, or unhappy.

The USA's older adults are more affluent, active, and satisfied with their lives than any generation before them. And
they're destined to remain a vital part of our nation in the
years ahead.

It's important to recognize that this trend is growing and
will likely reshape our national priorities, particularly as the
baby boomers get older. They'll have enough numbers and
financial clout to make the issues of the elderly the issues of
the nation.

What Is Old?

What is old? It seems like a relatively simple question. Or, at
least it did until we asked it of over 1,000 adults across the
USA in April 1986. Age, like beauty, is in the eye of the
beholder. The results we got depended entirely on the age of
the person answering.

- Among 25-year-old men and women, 65 was the average
  age they considered to be "old."
- To people in their 40s, age 72 is old.
- When we hit 60-year-olds, "old" jumped to 74.
- And among people 65 or over, 77 is old age.

Now, that's not as irrelevant as you might think—because
many of the problems the USA has in dealing with old people
come from not recognizing that multilayered perception of
what old really is.

The elderly are *not* one age group but several, and the people from 65 to 100 are not a whole lot more homogeneous
than the people from 30 to 65.

The "young old"—those age 65 to 75—are very active,
healthy, alert, alive, and involved. The "middle old-age"
group, age 75 to 85, also report a surprisingly vibrant and vital
life. Many of the problems you've read about really deal with
the "old old," those people 85 and older.

The problems of this last group are critical, because demographic bumps and medical breakthroughs are making this the fastest-growing group in the USA. They number 2.6 million now; that should double in the next 15 years.

And—hold on to your hats—in that same time period, the number of people over the age of 100, now about 32,000, should *triple*.

But it's the "young old" who seem to suffer most from the perception of old people as frail, immobile, and incapable.

"I don't feel like an old man," one 65-year-old man told us. And there's no reason he should.

More than ever, we're redefining in the '80s what it is to be elderly. And we're starting to shed the negative image that was implied so frequently in the '70s when we used the word "old."

More and more, we are understanding getting old as a movement into another stage of life, just as we moved from cradle to school, to work, to marriage, to parenthood. In outlook, health, and vitality, 65-year-olds today are more like the 55-year-olds of the past generation. And we will continue to push the age barrier back in the years ahead.

A doctoral student at the University of South Carolina responded to one of our polls. When we interviewed him in 1985, he had spent the previous four years sailing around the world teaching law, math, and history to U.S. sailors.

What made this man unusual for a student—but an archetype of what the future has in store—was that he was 69 years old.

Stayin' Alive

Many older people today are finding out that by staying productive they are staying healthy. Some have gone so far as to run successfully for a second term as president of the United States at age 73, but this is not something we would recommend to everyone.

At the beginning of the administration of Dwight Eisenhower (a spring chicken of 62 when he took office), more than four of every 10 men over 65 were in the labor force.

That's dropped by more than half. This has been a generation of telling people that 65 was the age to retire. That began as something of a dream, but for those wishing to remain active, it has turned into something of a nightmare. And very soon, we predict, it will change for a variety of reasons.

For many, being forced to retire means losing a sense of identity and self-worth they've struggled a lifetime to achieve.

Remember, we've seen that many different people in many different ways use their work to define themselves, and their sense of values. This need doesn't miraculously disappear as people get older or reach the "magic" age of 65.

A recent Louis Harris survey for the National Council on the Aging found over three-quarters of all workers 55 and over would prefer part-time employment to full-time retirement.

The good news is that the downturn in employing older workers should reverse itself fairly soon. A demographic shift taking place in the '80s will not only make more jobs available to the elderly, but also make the elderly more attractive to employers.

With the aging of the baby boom, the pool of younger workers—those under 24—will shrink drastically in the late '80s and early 1990s. Companies will be forced to encourage older workers to stay on the job—the same companies who now encourage workers to retire early.

Here's what we predict will happen in the 1990s: Companies will begin to offer more refresher courses and retraining, flexible scheduling, part-time work, or consulting work for special assignments, possibly even transportation to get older workers to the job. And these companies will be glad to have them. Some companies may even allow workers to retire a little at a time, perhaps working fewer hours or fewer days a week.

This will be a boon for the elderly. More than any other age group, the elderly tell us in our surveys that the satisfaction they receive from work is very important to them.

The Happiest Years

In studying results from thousands of interviews conducted for USA TODAY polls, one strikingly simple but vital fact stands out about the elderly; they are simply more at peace with themselves than other adults are.

There is, first, a simple reason for this. They have more money and are healthier than ever before, which means they can enjoy themselves longer. But there's a deeper reason, too. Old people are, quite simply, more satisfied with their place in life.

In several large studies, we asked adults about their hopes and desires, about what they liked and found wanting in life. Across the board, the elderly stood out. They are:

■ Least likely to say they don't have enough good friends.
■ Least likely to say they don't have time to do the things they want.
■ Least likely to complain about a lack of entertainment.

And there's more—much more.

Old people respect themselves more than any other age group does: They rate themselves higher when asked about how they fulfill their role in life as a husband or wife, as father or mother.

Old people are happier with where they live than anyone else; 74 percent of those 65 and older are very satisfied with where they live, compared with 58 percent of all adults.

Old people are the most likely group to say—as they have in survey after survey—that they're satisfied with the amount of fun in their lives. You do remember who are the least satisfied, don't you? That's right, it's those folks in the "prime of life," between the ages of 25 and 44.

In fact, when we compare the elderly to everyone else, the old folks say they're much happier with all sorts of things. For example, 84 percent are very satisfied with their friendships, compared with 74 percent of all adults. And 63 percent are very satisfied with their social lives compared with 52 percent of all adults.

Old people are more likely to feel liked and appreciated.
Here's one that will surprise you, and teach you something about self-respect in the Image Age: The elderly—both men and women—are more likely than people in *any other age group* to say they like the way they look. And this despite the fact that very few of them look like the people in the Levi jeans commercials.

Think old people complain a lot? Think again. Only 23 percent of those 65 and older say their life has gotten harder over the past year, compared with 33 percent of all adults.

They don't argue a lot, either. They're the least likely group in society to argue with their mates, and this is particularly true of arguments about job demands and financial matters, the exact things that younger people argue about most. And when old people do argue, they're the most likely to say that "both win."

Older people are, quite simply, more satisfied with their lives.

Feeling Good

Medical science and health care programs have helped to push back the problems of illness and frailty. The average life span today is 74 years, up from 47 in 1900. In fact, a 47-year-old today is hardly considered old.

Experts no longer believe that people must become senile if they live long enough. Disease, rather than simple aging, is now being seen as a more likely cause of senility, and we're conquering many of the diseases associated with senility.

The elderly are more concerned about their health than are younger people. They are more likely to watch their weight and eat properly. And this is having an impact. More than half of the elderly we polled—54 percent—say they are very satisfied with their health. This is exactly the same result we got when we asked all adults.

In addition, 53 percent say they are satisfied with their physical condition. Compare this with the response we get from the youngest adults, those 18 to 29; 56 percent say they are satisfied with their physical condition—statistically the same as for older folks.

Perhaps most important, old people are the least likely of any group to say they're under stress. They cite exactly half as much stress as those 18 to 24 when it comes to financial matters; and they cite half as much stress as those under 35 when it comes to making and keeping friendships. They cite less stress than other adults when it comes to trying to decide how to spend their free time.

And despite the fact that they're older, elderly people even complain less of stress than other adults when it comes to doing and sharing household chores.

Richer Than You Think

The elderly today have fatter wallets and more "disposable income"—money that's not tied up in paying bills—than any other age group in the nation. This ought to come as a surprise to some people who see the elderly as basically lonely and impoverished—and makes us wonder why Madison Avenue gears all its ads to the young.

The per capita income of households led by persons 65 or older is actually higher than for households led by persons under 50. They worked during a period of great economic vitality in the USA, and this has allowed many of them to accrue enough wealth to retire comfortably.

Again, we should stop here for a second. Many elderly people on fixed incomes are in a frightening position, unable to work and unable to get the assistance they need to make ends meet. This is a problem that the USA will have to pay particular attention to in the 1990s and beyond, as this group grows in size.

Given that proviso, consider these other statistics:

- Adults 55 to 65 have the highest per capita income in the USA, and those 65 to 75 have the highest average assets.
- Eight out of 10 elderly citizens describe their financial health as good.
- Most adults over 65 own their homes outright.
- 37 percent say they are *very* satisfied with their financial situation, compared with 23 percent of adults overall.

And old people are spending their money—a fact which, as we said, marketers are only belatedly starting to catch on to.

The elderly don't see themselves as frail and decrepit, but as confident and contented. We're already starting to see more advertising showing older people standing on their own, independent and free of the kids.

They represent an especially large market for luxury goods. They have more money to spend and fewer necessities to spend it on, since their day-to-day needs are diminishing as the family grows up. And, of course, they have more time; 75 percent say they have four or more hours per day to do with as they please, almost double that of most other age groups.

Some shrewd marketers see what is now being called the "mature market" growing:

- The elderly account for more than 70 percent of all "pleasure travel" dollars because they travel longer distances and stay away from home longer—a boon to the travel industry because of the rapid growth of retirees.
- Bus lines for years have offered discounts for older persons. Now airlines are doing the same thing.
- Producers are pitching food rich in calcium, which can help ward off diseases such as osteoporosis.
- Major retail and service companies are trying to attract older customers with club memberships and discounts on everything from car repairs to discount drugs.
- A store in Pennsylvania offers electric shopping carts with a seat and room for groceries to help make shopping easier.

We'll see more businesses catering to the elderly as more companies realize the importance of "the mature market."

This market will continue to grow and become more affluent as the baby boom generation ages. Over 60 million baby boomers will enter their 50s in the next decade. The number of households headed by elderly people with incomes of $50,000 or more is expected to rise by 50 percent by the mid-1990s.

The Young and the Old

There are two questions old people ask each other often. How often do you see your kids? Have you thought about going to live with them? So we decided to ask them, too.

One clear change in the USA through the last few decades has been the spreading out of the "extended family." This has accelerated tremendously since the 1970s as we've become such a mobile society.

It has become more and more rare for people to live in the same neighborhood as their parents, aunts, cousins, brothers, and sisters.

We were, however, pleasantly surprised to see that this problem is not quite as severe as we anticipated. In fact, it seems that people are making a strong if widely unpublicized effort to "go see the folks." For example, almost four out of every 10 teenagers say they see the grandparents every week; half see them at least a few times a month.

Teenagers: How often do you see your grandparents?	
Every week	37%
Few times a month	17
Once a month	14
Less than once a month	28
Never	4

We asked adults under 50 how often they see their parents. Again, nothing earth-shattering, but a pleasant surprise. More than 25 percent said they see their parents about once a day. This result, however, is somewhat deceptive—most of those were aged 18 to 29. Still, the results for other age groups were higher than you would think.

Adults under 50: How often do you see your parents?	
Every day	26%
A few times a week	18
Once a week	13
Two or three times a month	11
Once a month	8
Less than once a month	22
Never	2

Some people in the USA, of course, see their parents every day because their parents have come to live with them. The decision to have the parents move in is one that, people tell us, comes with enormous joys and enormous burdens.

Often it's the most agonizing question that people face about their parents as they age, one that many people think about for years and years: Should mom and dad move in? And when? Should I feel guilty for not inviting them?

Well, we asked young adults and older parents about this. And guess what? That's not the conflict at all. More often than not, the kids want mom and dad to move in when they get older, but the "old folks" prefer not to!

Our specific question: Should elderly parents move in with their children when the parents can no longer take good care of themselves?

A third of all adults agreed that was the best solution.

But here's what happened when we broke it down by age groups: Young adults were *more than twice as likely as old people* to say that their parents should move in. That's right: Among people 18 to 24, about half said that elderly parents should move in with the kids. But among people 65 and over, only one out of five thought it was a good idea.

The reason for this caught us by surprise, too—probably because we went into the study with the old stereotyped impressions of what old people think.

When we asked some elderly people why they didn't want to move in with their kids, we expected to hear them say that they didn't want to become a burden to their children. We heard some of that, but more often, we heard them say they didn't want to lose their independence.

The elderly aren't worried about their children. They're concerned about *themselves.*

Most elderly adults—three out of four—want to stay in a home of their own. And they feel that way even if they have to move to a different home, smaller or cheaper or easier to care for.

And, while almost 90 percent of all retirees still live in their own hometowns, more are starting to hit the road.

Between now and 1990, about 2 million are expected to move. The reason? Since they're healthier and more affluent, they're also more footloose.

Most common destinations included the 2,400 adults-only retirement communities in the USA—which, by the way, are not all in Florida or Arizona. Washington state is attracting retirees, as is the temperate climate of North Carolina. In fact, in 1960 North Carolina ranked 27th among states with elderly people migrating in; it has recently moved up to seventh.

Experts at a recent aging conference in Washington, D.C., agreed that many myths surround old age, and those myths need to be exploded. Among the myths they listed: When you're over 49, you won't feel healthy, think sharply, be interested in working, be sexually active, care how you look, or travel.

Said one, interviewed by USA WEEKEND: "We need to promote a more positive image of later life that reflects reality."

We found that all you need to do that for the elderly is simply to talk to them.

From people who are getting ready to finish up their work lives, our attention shifts now to people who are getting ready to start theirs.

CHAPTER ELEVEN

College Students

Want a glimpse into the future?

Take a look at the college students of today.

For many, college means being away from home—really away—for the first time in their lives, away from the influence of their parents and hometown friends. This is a chance to meet people with different thoughts and from different backgrounds. It is a time to build the attitudes and values they will carry for the rest of their lives, a chance to set their goals for the years ahead and to make decisions that will help shape the nation.

What goals are they setting?

As with previous generations, they're certain to become the leaders of our nation. More than 92 percent of the members of the U.S. Congress are college graduates, and most of the rest attended but didn't graduate. Seventy-nine percent of the founders of the fastest-growing companies in the USA are college grads, and 97 percent of the USA's corporate CEOs have attended college.

You don't have to attend college to be a leader in the business world, but it sure helps. They make up two-thirds of the managers in the nation's corporations.

To find out what college students are thinking now, and where the USA might be heading in the future, we conducted personal interviews with 1,000 students selected at random on 104 campuses across the USA.

The schools were carefully selected to be representative of all colleges. They ranged in size from tiny Nazareth College, a 1,372-student, Catholic Church-related school in Rochester, N.Y., to the giant University of Michigan, student body 38,000. They spread from the University of Massachusetts to the University of South California.

We found that many of the forces that are now starting to change the way we live in the home, the way we work, even what we think about the future—the forces we've been looking at throughout this book—will continue unabated. Indeed, some of these forces are likely even to intensify, cementing the changes that we see just starting to occur and altering forever the way we live in the USA.

We can expect that in the future:

- Women will continue to move out of the home to seek equality with men in the workplace.
- Our attitudes toward politics and business will continue to be conservative.
- Our attitudes toward sex and women's rights will continue to become more liberal.
- The vital importance of family life and children will remain firm.
- Perhaps most important, men and women will move toward the same goals for careers and family life and, we expect, learn to share more supportive, satisfying lives.

The vast majority of college students, men and women alike, plan to work and build careers. Unlike their mothers and older sisters, women in college are not headed toward traditional women's occupations, such as teaching. Yet, nine out of 10 women aspire to a marriage where both spouses work and share household chores. And a hopeful sign: Men appear to be placing a higher value on having children and on family life, including favoring a relationship in which they share the household responsibilities.

One thing will not change, however, despite the warnings of problems to come: the basic optimism that we feel toward the future.

Almost two-thirds, 62 percent, of the nation's college students believe they'll enjoy a higher standard of living than their fathers and their mothers. Of the rest, 30 percent say their lives will be just about as comfortable as those of their parents; only 7 percent said they don't expect to live as well as their mothers and fathers do.

This optimism is strongest in the minority community. Among blacks, 9 out of 10 say they'll be better off than their parents, significantly higher than for whites.

The optimism is also strong among the poor. Three out of four say they'll do better than their parents, much higher than among students whose parents are well-to-do.

On our survey we asked more than 150 questions on college life, issues facing the nation now and in the future, personal habits, attitudes toward work, money, and sex. Let's take a look at what college students are saying about where they're planning on taking us.

The Times They Are A'Changin'

The rise in protests over South African apartheid has been one of the more fascinating events on college campuses in the '80s, simply because the campus had seemed to become so calm through the 1970s. Students were telling their colleges to put political morality before financial considerations. Don't invest in companies that do business with South Africa, they said.

Mock South African "shanty towns" popped up on campuses across the USA. Prestigious Dartmouth hit the national headlines when members of the conservative *Dartmouth Review* decided to "clean up the green" and tear down the shanties. The results were sit-ins and teach-ins, as political flames of the '60s, doused for so long, seemed to be raging again.

How much have college students changed?

Put aside the question of just how radical the '60s really were, and whether any lasting change came from all those protests and sit-ins.

It seems safe to say that colleges were a focal point for liberal social change in the '60s. And according to our surveys, it also seems clear that the students of the '80s are less involved in changing the world than in improving their own lives.

Whether the seeds of protest that bloomed into the apartheid protests will continue to be sown is a question we'll have to watch as the decade winds down. As for now, there are few indications that it will.

Here's what we do know now: College students are becoming more politically conservative. Twenty-seven percent describe themselves as conservative, compared with just 15 percent on a similar survey conducted in the mid-1970s. Those considering themselves moderate to liberal have dropped from 85 percent to 72 percent.

Here's how they break down:

	1986	1975
Conservative	27%	15%
Moderate	42	54
Liberal	30	31

The shift becomes more obvious when we look at students' personal goals. The social conscience of the '70s is clearly taking a back seat to enterprise and entrepreneurism in the '80s. Today's students see college as a large investment in their future, and they plan to get a return, as big and as quickly as they can.

They're more interested in the bottom line than in social causes. As one writer described their unofficial motto in USA TODAY: "Plan for tomorrow. Live for today. Party tonight."

You can tell they're planning for tomorrow just by taking a look at what college students are majoring in today.

Major	Total	Male	Female
Business	19%	19%	19%
Engineering	11	15	6
Education	8	4	12
Biology	5	5	4
Science	4	5	3
Psychology	4	3	5
Communications	4	4	4
Computer Science	4	4	3
English	4	3	4
Political Science	4	5	3

English	4	3	4
Political Science	4	5	3

Education ranks third on the list with 8 percent. That's a huge shift from the mid-'60s when almost 25 percent, almost one out of four, college students were heading for some kind of a career in teaching.

Teaching hasn't become any less socially important, but it's been widely publicized that teaching generally doesn't pay too well. The return on their investment is too small to interest many of today's students.

When you look at the equal opportunity programs that started in the '60s, you see another possible indication of the college students' growing conservatism. We asked if they favor or oppose preferential treatment in hiring minority candidates to make up for racial imbalances in companies. Only 26 percent said they did, compared with 64 percent who disapproved.

Even among students identifying themselves as liberal, only a third endorse hiring to improve racial imbalances. Among blacks, these programs enjoy a majority, but not a mandate; 53 percent approve of it.

On the other hand, more liberal attitudes toward race seem to be emerging.

More than half of all students, 52 percent, say it wouldn't make any difference to them if they were paired with a roommate of another race. Most of the rest, 27 percent, say they would view this as a potentially positive experience, and 17 percent say they would accept it but would feel uncomfortable. Only 4 percent said they would ask for another roommate.

And even though students in the South are twice as likely as other students to say they would seek another roommate, that's still only 8 percent who say they'd do so.

The Typical College Student

Interest in fraternities and sororities may come and go on college campuses—right now it's growing. Styles in clothing may change, although jeans still top the list.

But one fact seems to stick forever. College students like to party.

Despite efforts to cut down on drinking on campuses across the nation, over 50 percent drink each week and about a third drink to excess every month. We'll fill in the details a bit later, but here's a quick sketch of college life '80s-style:

Jocks are still big men on campus, although most students feel sports are emphasized too much in college. Sex, drugs, and rock 'n' roll are still factors—although the sex and rock 'n' roll are holding their own better than the drugs, which are starting to fade out.

More than 15 percent of the USA's college students own computers. On dates, the men still usually pay. Many start smoking but many are also quitting. The love affair with cars stays strong. For the students who have one, it's the possession from which they get the most pleasure (the stereo comes second); for the students who don't, it's what they most want to buy.

Finally, they still look forward to getting out of school, but more than ever, it's so they can start working and making money.

Let's first look at a few demographic facts that are shaping the attitudes of today's college students and which, in turn, may very well affect our nation in the years ahead:

First, it's important to realize that Joe College is older these days. Believe it or not, the average college student is almost 22 years old. This may account for some of the growing conservatism on college campuses and for some of the decrease in drug use. And some government experts predict that by the early 1990s, more than half of all college students will be 25 or older.

In some cases, older students will be returning to school to upgrade their job skills or even receive career retraining. Others will work for a few years simply to decide exactly what they want to do with their lives, then go back to school for more education in that field.

It's also important to realize that over half of all students are women—52 percent by the mid-'80s, with the biggest jump coming from the group of women ages 25 to 34. We've already discussed the massive impact that women's educational progress is having in our society. There's no evidence to suggest that this won't continue and even grow in the decade ahead.

On an average day, the typical college student spends 1 hour and 54 minutes watching television, 3 hours and 49 minutes studying. And unlike high school, where our surveys showed that women did most of the studying, college men study just as hard, or at least as long, as women.

Almost two-thirds have some kind of job.

And what about the rest of their time?

College students love to socialize. Twenty-three percent say that's what they enjoy doing most when they're not in class.

What do they enjoy the most? Of our 1,000 college students, 2 percent said working. Watch them; they could be the Inc. 500 in the year 2000.

One percent said eating; 1 percent said running. Four students said they most enjoyed going to the beach (three were from California and one was from the Midwest); three said praying and 11 said making love.

Here's what they're doing when not in class:	
Socializing	23%
Listening to music	9
Reading	9
Sports	6
Sleeping	6
Exercising	5
Just relaxing	4
Watching television	3

When couples date, the boy still pays two-thirds of the time; only 2 percent of the women say they usually pay. But more and more they're splitting the cost: 25 percent of men and women say they usually split the cost of a date.

College students are a potent market. There are 12 million of them in the USA spending over $29 billion in discretionary income. They alone are responsible for buying one-fourth of all stereo components sold in the USA, more than 5 million pairs of running shoes, an ocean of beer, and, of course, jeans.

You can't talk college if you don't talk jeans.

Jeans are the equalizing force on college campuses, crossing political and economic boundaries. The average college man owns five pairs; women own six. There's no difference between liberals and conservatives, although moderates, for some odd reason, own more jeans. Kids from upper-income families also own more jeans than other students.

And speaking of clothes, women do spend more than men; 75 percent of the men and 61 percent of the women spend less than $500 a year on their wardrobe (which is surprising, considering the current cost of jeans). On the other end of the scale, 14 percent of the women spend more than $1,000 compared with 8 percent of the men.

Students do have money. They spend about $129 a month on the things they want. That's after necessities such as room, board, and tuition are paid for. Men spend more than women, about $56 a month more. Of course, there's always plastic money: 51 percent of USA college students have at least one credit card.

The most popular credit cards:	
Department store card	37%
Visa	21
Gas or oil company	17
MasterCard	14

And 97 percent said they left home without their American Express card.

All that discretionary income has posed something of a problem for marketers who are dying to get their hands on some of it. Since college students spend a lot less time than the average person in the USA watching television, marketers have lost one of their most potent tools, and have to get creative with their advertising.

They've come up with everything from special free magazines to posters and even videos to approach this attractive market. The verdict is still out, but one thing is certain: College students have money to spend, particularly since they're getting older, and companies aren't going to stop trying to get their hands on it.

Who pays the credit card bills? Three out of four college

students say they do; 12 percent say their parents pay, while 8 percent split the bill with mom or dad. The last are more likely to be women and more likely to be seniors.

On the other hand, it's usually the parent who pays for school bills such as tuition, room, and board.

Here's how the average college student's bills are paid:

Parents/other relatives	37%
Earnings from a job	21
Loan	14
Scholarship	11
Other student aid	9
Savings	5
Other	3

The average college student is in debt for about $4,084. An average of $689 of that is for a car, but most of the rest is for school loans, meaning the debt is much higher as we look from class to class. The average freshman's debt is $1,830; the average senior owes $5,943.

More than half of all college students, 56 percent, have tried smoking cigarettes—slightly more women, 58 percent, than men, 53 percent. The region with the highest percentage is the Northeast, where 65 percent have at least tried smoking; lowest is the South at 45 percent.

But only 41 percent of college students smoke now—again, fewer men than women, and almost twice as many in the Northeast as in the South. That's still higher than the national average (which is just over 30 percent) but it's dropping.

What else does the typical college student do? Fly, for one thing. More than half traveled by air in the last 12 months. They average just over three trips. For half of them, it was for a vacation or holiday. And don't be too sure the kids are coming home for Easter: 38 percent plan to go somewhere other than home or visiting relatives for spring break.

Where are the top spots to go to play? It depends on where you live.

Among students from the Northeast and Southeast, Florida easily rates No. 1. Half the students who don't go home tell us they head for the Sunshine State on spring break.

Who pays? Fifty percent say they saved the money from work. Mom and dad picked up most of the rest. And most of them will be singing "On the Road Again." Here's how they'll get where they're going for spring break:

Car or van	63%
Plane	31
Bus	4
Train	3

What doesn't a college student do?
Twelve percent have never cooked an entire meal; 26 percent have never balanced a checkbook; 40 percent have never made minor repairs to a car; 12 percent have never cleaned a bathroom; and 27 percent have never filled out an income tax form. On the other hand, 70 percent say they always do their own laundry.

OK. Two other interesting facts about the typical college student.

Among college students who don't live in their own hometown, about 25 percent talk to their parents every day. It will come as no surprise to parents, however, that freshmen call home about three times more frequently than seniors do.

And after college? A surprising 81 percent say they have already made up their minds about what kind of work they want to do after leaving school; that increases steadily from 72 percent of the freshmen to 89 percent of the seniors.

What job ranks No. 1?
What else—business.

Drinking, Drugs, and Partying

Drinking is as much a part of college life as ever, although the statistics on this have varied.

One of the problems here has always been that for many college students, drinking is illegal; for all of them, drugs are illegal—and it's hard to get accurate answers when you ask people if they've committed a crime.

So we approached this question in a slightly different way.

We asked students to tell us if their closest *friends* drink or use drugs. This seems to make people feel a little safer; and our experience is that phrasing questions this way yields a pretty good look at life on campus.

What the college students told us is that about two-thirds of their friends drink beer at least once a week. Just over half drink alcohol. A third of their friends drank to get drunk at least once in the last month. And there's no difference here between men and women.

What about drugs?
Eighteen percent say their friends have used marijuana and 5 percent have used cocaine.

We asked more directly about peer pressure to drink or use drugs, and a lot of students say there's a lot of it. Exactly half of both men and women say there is pressure from other students to drink in order to be part of college life. To a lesser degree, this is also true of drug use: One in five college students say there is pressure from other students to use drugs.

And you can't escape simply by going to another school. There's no difference in these answers on drugs and alcohol between religious and nonreligious affiliated schools. No difference by age of the students. No difference if they live in college housing, their own apartment or home, or with their parents.

Again, the only difference that shows up: Students in the South are slightly less likely to drink and use drugs, students in the Northeast slightly more likely.

College Athletics

The furor over college athletics reached a fever pitch in the spring of 1986 when a federal jury awarded $2.5 million to University of Georgia college instructor Jan Kemp, who claimed she was fired because she spoke out against preferential treatment for student athletes.

The verdict hinged on the question of free speech, but the controversy centered on whether colleges across the USA were going too far in "helping" athletes stay in school so they wouldn't be dropped from the team—efforts which, critics charged, ranged from remedial classes to grade-padding.

"I don't want [student athletes] knocking on my door five years from now offering to rake my leaves when they could have had an education," Kemp said.

In our studies, 51 percent of students say they feel college athletics are overemphasized. And the results are exactly the same for men and women.

And about the same number, half of all students, say athletes get preferential treatment on their campus; 38 percent say they don't. The rest weren't sure.

More than four out of 10 students say this preferential treatment takes the form of easier grading. About a third say it's easier for athletes to get into college in the first place.

Here's the full list of how many students say athletes get the following perks:

Easier grading	42%
Easier admission	34
Easier courses	24
Free meals	19
Better dorms or rooms	19
Payment of money	15
No work or little work jobs	12
A car	4

There's also very little support on campus for a proposal that comes up frequently: paying college athletes. A full 83 percent of the USA's college students say no, including 79 percent of the men and 88 percent of the women. Only 13 percent say athletes should be paid.

A Look Ahead

We wondered what these people who will be running the nation in a few decades think about the people who are running the nation now. We gave them a list of 15 major national institutions, ranging from the White House to organized labor. We asked them whether they have a "great deal of confidence," "some confidence" (kind of a ho-hum rating), or "hardly any confidence at all" in each.

The big winner is the medical profession. The big loser: labor unions. The White House evokes strong emotions—showing up on both the "pro" and "con" list, sort of the way

Howard Cosell used to be voted both the most loved and the most hated sportscaster in the USA.
Here are some of the results:

Profession	Percent citing a great deal of confidence
Medicine	58%
Colleges and universities	44
U.S. Supreme Court	47
White House	29
TV news	26
Congress	26

Profession	Percent citing hardly any confidence
Organized labor	29%
Organized religion	28
The press	21
Military	20
White House	17
TV news	17
Major companies	17
Law firms	17

It should come as no surprise that half of those who identified themselves as conservatives had a great deal of confidence in the White House, compared with 29 percent of all college students. Or that students at religious-oriented schools were almost twice as likely as others to say they had a great deal of confidence in organized religion.

It's a little disheartening for those of us in the press, however, to rate just a few points above lawyers and the state government when today's college students are asked about institutions in which they have a great deal of confidence.

Labor unions, however, did startlingly poorly, possibly another indication of the swing away from the days when Pete Seeger sang union ballads in college halls and Joan Baez roused Woodstock with a stirring version of a traditional ballad about organizer Joe Hill. In our poll, labor unions not only topped the list of institutions in which college students had little confidence, but came in dead last on the list of "high confidence" organizations.

Even among students who consider themselves liberal, only 15 percent say they have a great deal of confidence in unions, an indication of problems in the years ahead for organized labor in the USA.

Sex and Morality

While they may not be as politically conscious as their '60s counterparts, it appears that the sexual revolution is alive and well on the college campus.

This was another area we were afraid students might be reticent to talk freely about. To get the best, most accurate results we could, each of the 1,000 students we surveyed was given a questionnaire and an envelope in which to seal the responses to guarantee confidentiality.

Here's what we found:

Eight-five percent of the men and 65 percent of the women are sexually active. And of the students who are, about 58 percent lost their virginity between the ages of 16 and 18, in other words, just before entering college or soon afterward.

Among men overall, 71 percent enter college already "sexually active," according to the survey; by the time they're seniors, 83 percent describe themselves that way.

The change is greater among women: 48 percent say they're sexually active entering college, but 75 percent of seniors say they are. And the biggest shift in both figures comes in the freshman year.

Now, there's an upsetting figure to go along with that: Although 86 percent of men and women feel birth control is a shared responsibility—condoms and the pill are the two most-used methods of birth control—many sexually active students say they don't use any birth control at all.

Here's what kind of birth control method they use:

Men	
Prophylactic	37%
Withdrawal	19
Other	20
None	22

Women	
Pill	33%
Prophylactic	6
Diaphragm	6
Withdrawal	6
Sponge	4
Foam	2
IUD	1
Rhythm	1
Other	5
None	10

And here are the figures for when students say they lost their virginity:

Age	Men	Women
15 or younger	17%	6%
16 to 18	52	40
19 to 20	17	21
21	1	6
Over 22	1	2
Never	12	25

One more indication of the sexual liberation of today's college student: 23 percent have had a live-in romantic relationship with a member of the opposite sex (as you might expect, seniors are twice as likely to have done so as freshmen and students at church-related schools are about half as likely as other students). And 18 percent have shared a bedroom with a person of the opposite sex in their parent's home while their parents were in the house.

But while this sexual liberation seems to be fairly entrenched, questions of morality on sexual issues yield some fascinating contradictions—and offer glimpses into possible shifts in societal values. The questions we asked about were pregnancy, abortion, and homosexuality.

A little over half of all college students—53 percent—say it's all right for an unmarried woman to get pregnant if she wants to. Only 9 percent consider it shameful.

And a solid three-quarters of all college students feel that a woman less than three months pregnant should have the right to decide whether she wants to have an abortion. Almost two-thirds, 62 percent, say that it's a mistake to force a pregnant women to have a child.

But the answers are much less consistent when it comes to homosexuality. Although 81 percent say others' sexual preferences are their own business, 41 percent say homosexuality is wrong.

Why the contradiction?
The answer is men.
And this gives us a fascinating insight into the male thought process.

Almost half say homosexuality is immoral, more than a third higher than women. The reason, it appears, is that even at the age of supposed height of their masculinity men suffer from a fear of not appearing masculine. We've seen this same reaction in other surveys that we've done.

For example, we once did what we thought was a fairly innocuous write-in survey, in which we asked people of both sexes to choose the sexiest male and female athletes. While the women didn't hesitate at naming sexy women, the men balked at filling in the names of sexy men. Some simply left that section blank, but quite a few wrote in comments like: "How should I know? I'm not gay."

One last point about college students and their feelings about sex, one that is key to discussions of the matter as we move toward the '90s: Their fear of AIDS is growing greatly.

Almost half of all college students say they're more concerned about AIDS than they were a year ago, a testament to the impact and fear this disease is causing. Over a third say men and women should avoid casual sex because of the fear of AIDS, and that includes 45 percent of college women.

Work, Marriage, and Family

We've talked quite a lot about the changing place of women in society. What fascinated us most in the answers to our college student survey is not only how firmly college women have grasped the values behind that shift, but how college students—men *and* women—seem so thoroughly ready to embrace a new way of looking at their partners in life.

For it is a partner for life that college students want: 85 percent say they expect to get married, and in the not-too-distant future. They say the ideal age for a man to get married is 26, and 25 for a woman.

Whether those projections by students of their own futures will come true remains to be seen. Remember, people often say they're going to do one thing, but wind up doing another.

But judging from the values they express, it appears that a conflict between men's and women's goals in the '80s will wane sharply as these college students become adults.

Among adults in the '80s, we saw that most of the joys—and most of the problems—came from conflicts about "traditional" values. The strength and isolation of the workplace were the earmarks of the male in our surveys; work was his way of defining himself, but also his way of distancing himself from family concerns.

And for adult women, the family proved a conflict—how to move into the workplace without giving up the long-held belief that it was as a mother and wife that a woman defined her value to the world.

For men, it was the workplace; for women, the family.

What we appear to be seeing among college students is heartening. There seems to be much less difference between men and women when it comes to lifelong goals.

The vast majority of women plan to work and build careers. And a growing number of men are placing a higher and higher value on family life. It may be years before we find out if they really can live up to it, but it appears that college students are headed for a more harmonious time.

More than nine out of 10 women—92 percent—aspire to a marriage where both spouses work and share household chores. An encouraging if not quite equal 77 percent of men say they want just such a marriage. Only 6 percent of the women we talked to said they wanted to stay home while their husband works, and an ever-decreasing 15 percent of men say they want a wife who's a full-time housewife.

Finally, how many children will these liberated marriages produce?

Well, 88 percent say they want children (90 percent of the men and 86 percent of the women); 82 percent want two or more; and 39 percent want at least three.

Parents

For the child of the '60s, what is most noticeable about today's college students is the unabashed lack of disdain they feel for their parents' lifestyles.

There is no hint of cynicism in their answers when we asked students about how their parents lived and how they themselves want to live.

For one thing, college kids like their parents. And those of you who headed off to college in the 1960s and '70s humming "Come mothers and fathers throughout the land, and don't criticize what you can't understand"—sit down. A solid 68 percent of the USA's college students say their parents understand them quite well; only one in four feels misunderstood.

To catch a glimpse into the family of the '90s, we first asked students how they hope their lives will be different from those of their parents. The only two answers that emerged dealt with those same goals of work and family: They want to be financially better off and they want to have a better marriage. That's really about it; "I want to be more open-minded" was just about tied with "I don't want to be different at all."

How do you want your life to be different from your parents'life?

Better off financially	20%
Have a good marriage	12
Be more open minded	6
No way	5
Be more successful in work	4
Get a better education	4
Be happier	3
Work fewer hours	3
See more of the world	3

The most significant difference between men and women on this question: Women are 50 percent more likely than men to say they want their marriages to be happier than their parents'.

When we then asked how they would like their lives to be the same as their parents, the same goals came through: The top answers all dealt with family life and financial stability.

How would you like your life to be like your parents' life?	
Have a good marriage	18%
Have a good family life	12
Be just as happy	9
As financially stable	8
As successful at work	5

Some students also gave themselves a pat on the back: 7 percent said they wanted to raise good kids, just as their parents did.

And for those of you looking for the rebellious college youth, here they are: Only 3 percent of students said there is no way in which they wanted to be like their parents.

Getting Ready to Meet the World

We already know what kids are doing in college: getting ready to go to work. They should have no trouble fitting into the '80s lifestyle: they're career-minded; they're confident; they're ready to work long hours; and they're enormously eager to go out and try to survive in today's world.

More than nine out of 10 say their college did a good job preparing them to be successful in their chosen career.

Here's what they plan to do after college:

Work full time	44%
Go to graduate school	24
Work and go to school at the same time	16
Take a vacation	13
No plans	3

Of those going into the work world, 84 percent say they're excited about being out of school, although 49 percent admit the prospect makes them a little nervous.

When we asked for the *worst* thing about graduating, only 9 percent said, "I'll have to start working." The top answer here: 24 percent said leaving friends would be the worst thing about leaving school.

By way of contrast—and those of you who think college is just a place for goofing off ought to leave the room—35 percent of college students said joining the ranks of the gainfully employed was the best thing about leaving school. And a solid 81 percent know just what kind of work they want to do. In fact, 58 percent of those planning to go to work had gone on job interviews by the February before they graduated.

(By the way, 50 percent of men get a haircut for an interview—far surpassing the women—but about half of women buy something to wear to it, much more than men. What else can no job-hunting senior be without? Well, 28 percent had to get shoes; 6 percent bought books on how to interview; and 7 percent bought a briefcase.)

What's the first thing they plan to spend their money on? A car ranked No. 1: 39 percent plan to buy wheels. Getting their own place to live and a new wardrobe ranked next, well back at 14 percent.

By March of 1986, 26 percent of the students in the class of 1986 who intended to work already had accepted job offers. Their average weekly salary was $305.77. This should come as quite a surprise to those still looking; they expected to make a good deal more. The average weekly salary that college students say they expect to make on their first job is $446.34.

Seniors were smart enough to know, however, that they would have to work longer than nine to five to succeed. They expected to work an average of 44 hours a week—almost a nine-hour day. And 13 percent expected to work at least 50 hours a week.

Independence doesn't seem to be high on the minds of students when they think about leaving college, even though they're in for a big dose of it. About 9 percent called it the best thing about leaving college; an equally insignificant 7 percent called it the worst thing.

That might be related to this next response: A lot of them don't plan to go it alone. When we asked what kind of living arrangement they expect after college, here's what they said:

■ 28 percent expected to live alone.
■ 13 percent expected to live with their parents.
■ Among men, 28 percent expected to live with a male room-

mate and 3 percent expected to live with a woman.

- Among women, 28 percent expected to have a female roommate and 10 percent expected to live with a man.

Of course, many of our undergrads won't be leaving school at all when they graduate: About one in four intend to go to graduate school full time.

The first question we asked of people headed for grad school is why they're headed there. About half said they need it for their hoped-for career—such as in medicine or law.

Most of the rest, 38 percent, say they don't *have* to go to grad school, but that it will help them be more successful in their careers.

And here's a telling note about our changing society: Women were twice as likely as men to say they were going to graduate school to help assure success in their career. Only 25 percent of men said their main reason for going to graduate school was that it would eventually make them more successful, but 55 percent of women said this was what is motivating them.

This undoubtedly reflects that growing trend we saw toward women making success at work a greater goal in their lives.

And maybe it also shows a realistic response to the sexism of the work world. College women may perceive that they'll need the extra credential of a graduate degree to get their fair share in the marketplace.

Just to round out the reasons for graduate school: 9 percent say they want more education until they decide on their career, and 3 percent say they just flat-out like school and don't want to leave yet.

And to wrap it up, here are the top career goals for students headed to grad school:

Medicine	19%
Law	15
Business	10
Education	6

The USA in the Years Ahead

College students feel there's good news and bad news ahead for the nation.

Nine out of 10 college students believe U.S. troops will be sent abroad to act as "peacekeepers" (i.e., a situation similar to the role we played in Lebanon) sometime over the next 10 years; and half say we're likely to be involved in a Vietnam-style war. The good news, if you can call it that, is that only one in 10 say we'll kill ourselves in a global nuclear war; that's less than half the number of high school students and slightly less than the number of adults who feel this way.

However, only 31 percent say they expect the world to be more at peace in 10 years than we are now. The results don't vary by political bent, region, or parents' income. There are some interesting differences, though: Black students are much more pessimistic about nuclear war—three times more likely than whites to expect a nuclear war.

Men are generally more optimistic than women; they're a third more likely to say we'll enjoy peace in the years ahead.

If you haven't noticed by now, this sex difference is true in almost all our surveys, not just among college students and not just on this subject. In almost every aspect of life men are more optimistic than women.

Women are just as optimistic as men about their own futures, but they're almost always more concerned about the future of others, whether we're talking about the stability of the family, the future of the economy, or the prospect of war.

That may be one reason that women overall show less confidence than men do in the direction of our nation and its leaders. Specifically, women have less faith in Ronald Reagan than men do.

These questions—war, peace, and Ronald Reagan—are, as we'll see in a later chapter, central to understanding the '80s and where we're going to be as a nation by the time these college students take over.

First, however, let's take a break and look at some of the ways we play and entertain ourselves.

CHAPTER TWELVE

The USA at Play

Now let's have some fun.

What do you daydream about the most? Travel and vacation top the list. In fact, one in five people who daydream say they dream about going places and not working. Following—and not very close behind at that—are wealth and success on the job.

If your son were a college football player, where would you most like him to play? Penn State and Notre Dame topped the list. No other schools came close. The big reason parents gave: academics, overwhelmingly.

Which celebrity are you most tired of? Well, here are the answers:

Howard Cosell	21%
Ed McMahon	17
Brooke Shields	16
Joan Rivers	14
Mary Lou Retton	13
Joan Collins	11

In this chapter we're going to take a break and look at the kinds of things you do when you take a break.

Of course, this chapter isn't *all* fun and games. We here in the USA take our sports and our entertainment very seriously, and those topics raise some serious questions, especially if you're a parent trying to decide which is the best sport for your children to play.

And sports and entertainment are *very* serious topics for the people who make money off them. Leisure is a big business, bringing in billions each year. It's a business that will expand in the decades ahead: More working couples means more income to spend on the things we want. And a little further down the road, more old people (remember the aging baby boom) means more free time to have fun with.

And sports and entertainment are serious because we're a funny kind of people here in the good old USA, where our ways of taking our leisure sometimes aren't so leisurely at all. Just consider these examples:

SEIZE THE DAY OFF: We asked people to rank their favorite leisure activities. Participant sports ranked No. 1. It was the top choice of one out of three people overall, and two out of five of all men. "Relaxing" came in well down the list.

Here are the top choices:

Sports	33%
Fishing or hunting	12
Reading	12
Hobbies	11
Relaxing	6

And we may even be sneaking more work into our play than the figures show. The reading is often work-related.

We view leisure as a time to recharge our batteries, but also a time to catch up on our chores. And 55 percent of us say we engage in "vigorous" sports at least once a week; 39 percent of all adults say that's at least three times a week. And almost three out of four, 72 percent, say they plan to get more exercise.

Changes in lifestyles have made our leisure activities more fast-paced, more frequent, and certainly more competitive. Time-conscious, goal-oriented Americans work hard, even when they play.

We hit golf balls, always striving for the perfect swing. We jog, working on each run to better the time on our preceeding jaunt. We strive to reach the perfect bowling score and we pursue the inner game of tennis.

Active pursuits like bicycling and other sports have all increased. More serene pursuits like taking a drive in the country or picnicking have all fallen off in the '80s.

PUT ON A HAPPY BUT EFFICIENT FACE: Fun is fun, all right, but work is important. Half of us say the time we spend at whatever we call leisure is not as important as work.

The rest, at best, call it a tie.

Why do we have so much trouble taking it easy?

A lot of it has to do with '80s life, and there's no evidence that this particular aspect of this decade will change in the '90s. Remember, we learned early on that six out of 10 of us say we don't have enough time to do the things we want, and the percentage is even higher for baby boomers. When we do spend time on anything outside of work, it has to feel important to us, as though time is a terrible thing to waste.

In personal interviews, people indicate that more and more they're treating time as a commodity. And they want maximum return for their investment, like the man who told us in one interview that he gets up early on weekends "to get his golf out of the way" so he can get his work done.

THREE DAYS OF THE CONDOR, MAYBE FOUR: Sixty percent of all adults now tell us that they prefer to take several short trips rather than one longer one. The three- and four-week vacation is becoming more and more unusual—a victim of the press of business in the fast-paced '80s.

Some people said they simply didn't want to "blow" their vacation on one long trip, but many people simply don't want to be away from work that long.

Another factor is the increasing number of working couples. It's difficult for working couples to match up big blocks of time to take off together.

This, too, is a trend we see continuing into the '90s. If the travel and leisure industry is smart, it will plan and promote these four- and five-day mini-getaways (and if they're really smart, they won't forget about the kids).

JUST YOU AND ME . . . Most married people (90 percent) take their spouses on vacation, although one in five admit taking a trip without their spouse.

. . . AND BABY MAKES THREE: In seven out of 10 households in which children live, the kids come along for the vacation. The percentage is higher for women than for men, largely because of the larger number of divorced or separated mothers taking care of the children.

For those traveling with kids, 69 percent said the children were an important consideration behind the decision on where to go on vacation. This ought to be kept in mind as the number of families with small children increases each year as a result of the "baby boom echo."

WITH FRIENDS ON WEEKEND VACATIONS: Nineteen percent are traveling with friends of the opposite sex. And here's a surprise: Those most likely are not young adults but those in their late 30s. And they're much more likely to be divorced. There are also 2 percent of married adults who said they are traveling on vacation with a friend of the opposite sex. But we won't tell anybody.

LIBYA IS DEFINITELY OUT: Fourteen percent of all adults have ruled out visiting a specific location they were considering for vacation because they are worried about terrorism against U.S. citizens. This is particularly high since a large percentage of the remaining 86 percent were not in the market for foreign travel anyway. Europe, particularly Greece, was the location most often named.

IT'S A BIRD, IT'S A PLANE, IT'S SUPERSAVER: Cheap air fares have also become a lure for many; 17 percent of all adults said they have taken a trip recently just because of the cheap air fares. Top locations: California for the West; Florida for the Northeast.

DEFINITELY, ANYWHERE BUT LIBYA: Finally, we asked people to dream. If money were no object, where would you go on vacation? The 1,000 people surveyed named 138 different locations, from Monaco to Kansas City, from Nashville to Portugal, from Palm Springs, Calif., to Lake George, New York. Libya was not on the list.

Here are the top dream spots:

Hawaii	28%
Europe	9
Australia	5
Florida	5

California	5
Bahamas	4
Caribbean	3
Alaska	2
Colorado	2

LET'S DO LUNCH: Which entertainment celebrity would you most like to meet?

Bill Cosby	13%
Bob Hope	12
Clint Eastwood	11
Kenny Rogers	10
Tom Selleck	9
Barbra Streisand	8

BUT DO WE HAVE TO HAVE JELL-O FOR DESSERT? Which entertainment celebrity makes you laugh the hardest? Cosby scores another hit.

Bill Cosby	28%
Eddie Murphy	18
Bob Hope	13
Richard Pryor	12
Johnny Carson	9
Chevy Chase	9
Joan Rivers	8

YEAH, I LIKE THE SHOW; IN FACT, I JUST HAD LUNCH WITH THE GUY: Now, we asked this when his show was the top-rated one on TV, and maybe people have short memories, and don't tell Lucy this, but when we asked people for their favorite TV show of all time . . .

Cosby Show	16%
M*A*S*H	13
Miami Vice	8
Dynasty	7
60 Minutes	7
Hill Street Blues	6
Dallas	6

Cheers	5
Star Trek	5
Gunsmoke	4

E.T., STAY HOME: What's your favorite movie of all time? Frankly, my dear, this shouldn't be much of a surprise. Despite the success of *E.T.: The Extra-Terrestrial*, the Star Wars saga, and the never-ending tale of Rocky Balboa, *Gone with the Wind* is easily our top choice. It's interesting to note—especially in light of the TV poll we just mentioned—that when we asked people in 1986 to name their favorite movies, the winners were made an average of 21 years ago.

Here are the top vote-getters and the year they were made:

Gone with the Wind (1939)	23%
The Sound of Music (1965)	11
E.T. (1982)	10
Rocky (1976)	9
Dr. Zhivago (1965)	9
Casablanca (1942)	7
Star Wars (1977)	7
Love Story (1970)	5
The Way We Were (1973)	5

DON'T BE CRUEL: Maybe everybody else was out at Graceland the day we conducted this poll, but Elvis came in second when we asked you to name your favorite singer of all time:

Kenny Rogers	14%
Elvis Presley	11
Lionel Richie	10
Bruce Springsteen	10
Barbra Streisand	9
Bing Crosby	8
Perry Como	7
Loretta Lynn	6
Frank Sinatra	5
Willie Nelson	5

THE WORLD SERIES OF TELEVISION: In which areas does television programming to its best job? The television people got few rave reviews. Here's what you say:

Rating as excellent	Percent
Special sports events	48%
News specials	35
Nightly news	31
Regular sports programs	30
Special dramatic series	21
Nightly entertainment shows	6

STRIKE THREE: Which would you prefer to watch on television: professional baseball or professional football? Pro football wins by two field goals and a safety. Almost half, 49 percent say football; 41 percent say baseball.

AND THE REST WERE BUSY WATCHING THE ROLLER DERBY: Despite the hitting and the pounding, only 28 percent say there's too much violence in professional football; 64 percent say it's OK.

EXCEPT ONE IS MUCH LARGER THAN THE REST: What sports celebrity would you most like to meet? There's really no difference among the top three choices:

Joe Montana	13%
William "The Refrigerator" Perry	12
Mary Lou Retton	12
Joe Namath	11
Chris Evert Lloyd	10
Walter Payton	9
Dan Marino	8
Jack Nicklaus	7

MONTANA SCORES A TOUCHDOWN: Who is the sexiest male sports celebrity? (We used answers from women only here):

Joe Montana	22%
Joe Namath	18
Dan Marino	16
Steve Garvey	11
George Brett	5
Marcus Allen	2

CHRISSIE SERVES, JANE RETURNS THE VOLLEY: This time we took only men's answers. The question: Who is the sexiest female sports celebrity?

Chris Evert Lloyd	26%
Jayne Kennedy	26
Mary Lou Retton	16
Jan Stephenson	11
Carling Bassett	4

A CAPITAL IDEA: Which city deserves a baseball team the most? The nation's capital, Washington, D.C. Followed by Denver, Miami, Indianapolis, and Phoenix.

OF COURSE, BOTH WOULD BE NICE: What is your favorite ballpark food? Hot dogs by a long shot, at 61 percent; chased by a beer, 8 percent.

THEY JUST DON'T GIVE AWAY MANY STEINWAY PIANOS ANYMORE: What's the best ballpark freebie you ever got? Nine percent said a cap, 8 percent said tickets, 8 percent got a baseball.

DAY OF THE DOLPHIN: Who's the best professional football coach? Miami Coach Don Shula tops easily with 43 percent followed by San Francisco coach Bill Walsh, 18 percent. Next: Dallas' Tom Landry, Pittsburgh coach Chuck Noll, and Chuck Knox of Seattle.

DID YOU SAY PLAY A ROUND OR PLAY AROUND? With whom would you most like to play a round of golf? Two of the game's legends topped the list: Arnold Palmer and Jack Nicklaus. Next? Golf's glamour girl, Jan Stephenson.

CALLING A FOUL: Which sport has the worst officiating?

Basketball	36%
Football	22
Hockey	9
Wrestling	8
Baseball	6

WELL, FOR ONE THING, SHE'D CATCH HER DEATH OF COLD IN THAT SKIRT: Would you like your daughter to be a cheerleader?

Yes	28%
No	56
Not sure	16

GOING FOR THE GOLD: We asked a long series of questions about the Olympics. You'll see some of these same questions popping up in the next few years as we get ready for the 1988 games.

First we asked: Would you want your son or daughter to be an Olympic athlete? That's easy enough, right? Who would say no? Well, about a third of you did, surprising us.

Would you want your son or daughter to be an Olympic athlete?

Yes	61%
No	33
Not sure	6

KEEP THE POLITICS OUT: Are the Olympic games too political? An overwhelming majority said yes.

Yes	84%
No	10
Not sure	6

KEEP THE USA IN: Even though we think the games are too political, most of us think the USA should remain in them.

Should the USA drop out of the Olympic games?

Yes	16%
No	77
Not sure	7

KEEP THE PRIDE UP: One reason we want the USA to stay in the games: We think the Olympics have a positive impact on our prestige around the world.

A great deal	33%
Some impact	46
Little impact	16
Not sure	5

PASSING THE HAT: Most of us don't feel the federal government should subsidize our athletes, as they do in some other countries. We're more likely to say business should help, but overwhelmingly, people in the USA say they themselves should be the ones to support our athletes.

Should the U.S. government provide financial support to Olympic athletes directly out of regular tax revenues?

Yes	32%
No	62
Not sure	6

Should USA companies be allowed to pay Olympic athletes?

Yes	41%
No	50
Not sure	9

Would you donate $1 to help USA Olympic teams?

Yes	70%
No	25
Not sure	5

(Which again tells us that sometimes people say one thing and do another, because if 70 percent of us donated a dollar to the Olympic team we wouldn't be asking this question in the first place.)

Despite the problems of getting money and despite the fact that many foreign athletes are, in fact, professionals, most of us don't feel our professional athletes should be allowed to participate; 35 percent said yes, 58 percent said no.

A PERMANENT HOME: We also asked about a proposal you hear frequently: to hold the games in a permanent location, like Greece, to cut down on political disruptions such as the U.S. and Soviet boycotts that have marred recent games.

Should the Olympics have a permanent home?

Yes	43%
No	49
Not sure	8

GO FOR THE GOLD? I'D RATHER GO FOR A WALK: How about you? Would you like to participate in the Olympics? Here's a surprise: Most say no.

Would you want to participate in the Olympic games?

Yes	36%
No	63
Not sure	1

Now let's look at what we think about our kids and everyday sports.

THE LITTLE RASCALS TAKE THE FIELD: We think there's too much pressure in high school sports; nevertheless, an overwhelming majority of us are convinced that sports help to build character and fitness in our youth.

More than half of adults, 54 percent, participated on a high school athletic team of some sort—70 percent of the men and 36 percent of the women. And more than 30 percent have at least one child who participates on a high school team.

- 62 percent of all adults say there's too much pressure in high school sports today.
- 82 percent say sports help keep kids out of trouble by keeping them off the street.
- 30 percent say there's too high a risk of injury in high school sports today.
- 22 percent say too much tax money is spent on high school athletics.
- 77 percent say sports teach children valuable things about life that they cannot learn in the classroom.
- 92 percent say sports contribute to the health and fitness of youth.

Is there too much emphasis placed on high school sports in your community?

Too much	30%
About right	50
Too little	13

WATCHING ON TV IS ONE THING, BUT . . .: Football, the big crowd-pleaser and money-maker, is one of the sports parents are least likely to encourage their children to play. Take a look at how parents compare the different sports.

Question: Would you encourage or discourage your children from participating in any of the following sports?

	Encourage	Discourage
Swimming	93	2
Baseball	89	5
Tennis	89	5
Basketball	87	7
Golf	76	15
Soccer	71	21
Football	54	40
Wrestling	48	44

MAYBE WE SHOULD ASK THE WASHINGTON SENATORS TO INTERVENE: Should teams be legally prohibited from moving if their fans object?

The question is sure to come up in the years ahead, just as it did in the mid-'80s when the former owner of the Philadelphia Eagles threatened to move the team to Phoenix and after the Baltimore Colts moved to Indianapolis. As the 1986 season started, New York Yankees fans were trying to discourage their team from following other New York teams to New Jersey.

Most people don't think teams should be prohibited from moving, but they do think the owner should be required to make a legitimate attempt to sell the team locally before carting it off to some distant city. Here's what you said:

Should owners should be prohibited from moving their teams?

Yes	28%
No	51
Not sure	21

Should a team owner be required to make a legitimate attempt to sell the team to people in the community before moving a team?

Yes	59%
No	27
Not sure	14

TAKE ME OUT TO THE *&!!#@*#! BALL GAME: We saw an ugly side to sports in the '80s, which also, unfortunately, shows little sign of waning. The violence, the profanity—and that's not taking into account what happens *on* the field.

Drinking and violence have become a real problem in the stands. To counter this, several stadiums have stopped selling beer late in the games, and others have established "family sections" so fans with children can band together in one area.

To explore the seriousness of the problem, we first asked people who had attended sporting events a series of questions about their experiences:

- More than one-third of all sports fans, 37 percent, say there are sporting events they would not take their family to because of foul language and rowdy behavior by fans.

Which sports would they avoid?

Wrestling	65%
Hockey	52
Football	29
Basketball	22
Baseball	20

- 43 percent say that when they're at the ballpark there is excessive drinking in the stands around them. Among people who attend sporting events most frequently, that rises to more than 50 percent.

AND THEN OF COURSE THERE'S NO INSTANT REPLAY: About a third of the sports fans we interviewed say they are attending fewer games in person. Here are their most frequently mentioned reasons:

Can watch enough sports on TV	51%
Too expensive	36
Rowdiness in the stands by fans	14
Too busy	13
Favorite team not winning	11

TAKING OFF THE GLOVES: Boxing gets a split decision; about half of all adults want to leave the sport as it is and half want a ban of some sort because of the violence involved. Of those who want a ban:

■ 85 percent want a total ban on the sport.

■ 10 percent oppose professional boxing only.

■ 5 percent want amateur boxing outlawed.

It might come as no surprise, but twice as many women as men want to ban boxing.

THE TOTALLY BANANAS BOWL: More than two-thirds of all adults think it's time to change the way we pick the "unofficial No. 1 college football champion." Almost three out of four men, 72 percent, and 60 percent of women, want college football to choose a national champion through competition—rather than the writers' and coaches' polls that are used now.

OK, break time's over. Now let's take a look at one football fan in particular, and the way he's changed the sport of politics—maybe forever.

CHAPTER THIRTEEN

Reagan, Patriotism, and the Government

They start early each morning on the roof of the Capitol building in Washington, D.C. A team of workers runs a flag up a flagpole, pauses for 30 seconds, and then hauls it back down. Then they take another flag and do it again. And again—all day long if the weather is good. They average 200 flags a day, one every 2 minutes and 15 seconds.

The flags are then boxed and sent by members of Congress to friends and constituents all over the USA. And each can proudly, and rightfully, claim to be the possessor of a flag that had flown over the nation's capital.

The demand for these flags has risen by 34 percent over just the past four years; a fitting symbol, perhaps, of our time.

Our research clearly shows that patriotism, in some form—whether it's a simple desire to wave the flag or something much deeper—is on the rise.

But this is a different kind of patriotism from the patriotism of the 1940s, when we loved our country because the rest of the world seemed so wrong and out of whack. Or the patriotism of the '50s, when we loved our country because everything in it was so right.

Or 15 years ago, when the flag was a symbol of a different sort, often worn upside down on the seat of one's jeans as a protest.

And in many ways this is also a more tolerant patriotism, confident, yet ready to accept some doubt. You don't have to love-it-or-leave-it any more.

It is very simple patriotism, personified to a large extent by one man, Ronald Reagan. And it is a very complex patriotism: Bruce Springsteen poses before an American flag on his album cover and sings "Born in The USA," a bitter anthem about the plight of the Vietnam veteran. It is embraced by liberals angry at the government—and praised by conservative George Will.

Reagan himself calls Springsteen a great hero; Springsteen hints that perhaps Reagan didn't hear the whole song. Who wins the right to wave the flag here? Who is the patriot? Reagan? Springsteen? The Vietnam veteran?

Maybe all of them.

In this chapter we'll look at this rebirth of the spirit and at some of the forms it is taking. We'll also take a careful look at Reagan, who without a doubt is the center of this patriotic surge. Finally, we'll delve into the issues and problems facing the USA now and in the years ahead.

The Pride Is Back

Red, white, and blue turned fashionable in the mid-'80s. You can see it in our newspapers and magazines, hear it in the music and in the jingles, read it on the faces of our people, young and old, who are no longer reticent to stand up and salute the flag. Listen to the National Anthem the next time you are at a ballpark. Look at the people around you as they sing it. Something is clearly happening.

The new patriotism marks an end to, or maybe comes as a backlash to, more than a decade of national doubt that started when the U.S. pulled out of Vietnam and Nixon pulled out of the White House.

We were shocked and horrified at the sight of U.S. helicopters fleeing from the top of the U.S. embassy in Saigon. For many it was the first realization that the good old USA really could fall short. My country right or wrong, we realized, might have been wrong.

Watergate told us our leaders were fallible. The hostage

crisis in Teheran told us our people were vulnerable. The recession told us our nation, literally and figuratively, wasn't working.

Now, however, to steal a phrase from one of the popular new ads of the '80s—"The Pride Is Back."

It was an unabashed, exaggerated brand of chauvinism. In the movie *Red Dawn*, a group of high school kids fight an invading Soviet-Cuban army to a virtual standstill "in the early days of World War III." Add to that Chuck Norris' *Invasion USA*, and *Rambo*, and the cumulative impact was so fierce that some Soviet officials complained the movies were designed to foster anti-Russian passions.

Imagine how Katya Lycheva, the 11-year-old Soviet girl who visited the USA in 1986, felt when she watched *Rocky IV* and saw a bloodied Sylvester Stallone stand triumphantly draped in the U.S. flag after vanquishing a nearly super-human Russian boxer.

The business community, as always, knew a good thing when they saw it—the Statue of Liberty couldn't have picked a better time to celebrate her 100th birthday, and she showed up in ads for everything from cameras to jewelry. G.I. Joe became part of a popularity sweep as strong as the sentiment against it in the early '70s—when it was condemned as too violent a toy for children.

But behind this fantasy-patriotism of Rambo going back to refight the Vietnam War singlehandedly, our surveys found a patriotism that is undoubtedly strong and getting stronger—but tempered by reality. Let's look at the results of some of the questions we asked people recently about patriotism and then look at what this might mean for the future.

Cheers for the Red, White, and Blue

First, we wanted simply to see if this trend really was developing, if we're more patriotic than we were a decade ago, back when Gerry Ford was president, the nightmare of Watergate was over, and we were preparing to celebrate the nation's bicentennial.

Without offering a definition of "patriotism"—letting people attach whatever values to the word they wanted—we asked simply: Do you think that people are more patriotic

about the USA now than they were 10 years ago? Here are the
responses:

More patriotic	43%
Less patriotic	24
About the same	30
Not sure	3

By a ratio of almost 2 to 1, people are more likely to say that
patiotism in increasing than decreasing. So then we asked
people about themselves specifically: Are *you* more patriotic
about the nation now than you were 10 years ago? Half said
they felt about the same; but as for the rest:

Are you more patriotic than you were 10 years ago?	
More patriotic	39%
Less patriotic	8

That's a ratio of almost five-to-one. Now, those of you who've
been following all along figure there are more old people than
there used to be, so that must make up the difference, right?

Wrong. The people most likely to say they're getting more
patriotic are young adults—by an overwhelming margin.

More than half of those 18 to 24 say they're more patriotic
now.

We also found an abiding faith in the principles on which
the USA grew. One, for example, is the belief in the future and
that the Horatio Alger story can still come true—further
proof, we feel, that the doomsayers are wrong, that the USA
still has a bright future. We asked:

Can anyone still make it in the USA? Or, put another way, is this still the land of opportunity?	
Yes	86%
No	10
Not sure	4

This confidence was shared by men and women alike, people
of all ages and educational backgrounds. And even among the

poor, eight out of 10 say the USA is still the land of opportunity. They feel that anyone can still start from nothing and still become a success.

Then we asked people how they thought the country was changing and how it would change in the decades ahead.

We found that despite the wars and the recessions, the problems and the protests that we have lived through, people by and large feel the U.S. is a better place to live now than 25 years ago. That was 1961, John F. Kennedy was president and Camelot was in full bloom. More than two-thirds, 68 percent, feel life is at least as good and exactly half say it's better. Here is what you said:

Is the USA a better place to live today than it was 25 years ago?	
Better	50%
Worse	23
Same	18
Not sure	9

And what about the future? We're less certain here, and that's due largely to the dark threat of war that stays with us in the nuclear age. Nevertheless, we generally feel optimistic about the future, and are more likely to say things will get better than we are to expect them to get worse.

In 25 years, will the USA be a better place to live than it is now?	
Better	38%
Worse	21
Same	28
Not sure	13

Our final question in this series was a little less straightforward—and yielded answers a little less one-dimensional. What we asked was:

If the USA's founding fathers could see the nation today, would they be proud or disappointed?	
Proud	54%

Disappointed	38
Not sure	8

By a fairly solid margin we feel our founding fathers would be proud—but far from a landslide.

It's on questions like these that we found the nation, while increasingly patriotic, nevertheless in a "sorting out" process. Unlike the '50s, people today are less likely to say everything we do is right. Unlike the '70s, people today are less likely to say everything we do is wrong.

We're realizing that the USA does many things right and some things wrong. That's a healthy introspection that may very well leave us better suited to meet the rigors that lie ahead in the 21st century.

Certainly, things have changed since 1979 when President Jimmy Carter warned the nation about "a crisis of confidence . . . that strikes at the very heart and soul of our national will."

That there has been an upswing in the spirit is almost without question. You could see it in the way we honored our dead back from the bombing of the Marine Corps barracks in Lebanon, and in the way we reacted to the invasion of Grenada. In the massive celebration that became the Los Angeles Olympics we even seemed to forget that the Soviets were missing. There was a unity in the national experience—unity in joy when Mary Lou Retton won the gold, unity in our tears in the tragic loss of the space shuttle Challenger—and unity in resolve that the space program should continue. Indeed, seven out of 10 say it should continue.

Most recently, we saw this unity in the spring of 1986 when Libyans fired on U.S. planes operating over international waters. The U.S. fired back, destroying Libyan ships and attacking a missile site.

Two-thirds of all adults—a full 67 percent—backed the military retaliation even though the Libyans damaged none of our planes and although a clear majority of us felt the action increased the chances of terrorism against U.S. citizens around the world.

Most significantly, however, 83 percent agreed with this statement: "I'm glad that the USA is standing up for its rights around the world, even if it means taking some military risks."

Again, the huge majority who agree with such a statement belies the complexity of our feelings about war, Reagan, and Ramboism. The image that these results can conjure up—of a nation blindly following Ronald Reagan wherever he and his Joint Chiefs of Staff wish to take us—is simply not true.

For example, 69 percent ranked President Reagan's handling of foreign policy as good or excellent. But only a third agree with him that the USA should provide military aid to the contras fighting to overthrow the Sandinista government in Nicaragua.

What seems clear is that the people of the USA are tired of their nation being thought of as an impotent giant—but that they think twice about becoming too deeply involved in the internal struggles of other countries.

Then again, while Reagan lost out on that Nicaragua poll, let's take a look at a few others—because he hasn't lost out on too many.

Papa Ron

Ronald Reagan didn't win his second term on Nov. 6, 1984, even though that's the day voters went to the polls. He won it exactly 53 weeks earlier, on Oct. 27, 1983.

Under fire for his handling of the U.S. peacekeeping efforts in Lebanon—more than 241 U.S. troops were dead or dying after the bombing of their headquarters in Beirut—and his decision to invade the tiny Caribbean island of Grenada, Reagan chose to go on national television. He wanted to take his case directly to the people.

The speech, our surveys soon showed, would change the course of U.S. history and ensure Reagan's re-election. They also showed the immense power Ronald Reagan had over the people when he could talk to them through the medium he had made his own—television.

In just 30 minutes Reagan broke the growing opposition to his policy in Lebanon and turned the modest support he already enjoyed over Grenada into a landslide.

"The president was beginning to develop a significant liability in foreign affairs," said pollster Gordon S. Black of Rochester, N.Y.

"With this one speech he turned that liability into an asset."

We conducted two polls, one before and one after Reagan's speech. The differences were amazing.

Before the speech: 39 percent agreed with Reagan's decision to send the Marines to Lebanon.

After the speech: 53 percent approved.

Before the speech: 48 percent said the Marines should remain in Beirut.

After the speech: 59 percent approved.

Before the speech: 48 percent of the USA's adults approved of the Grenada invasion.

After the speech: 68 percent approved.

Before the speech: 21 percent of the registered voters said they were "more likely to vote for Reagan because of his decision to invade Grenada."

After the speech: 32 percent were more likely to vote for him because of Grenada.

Before the speech: 47 percent said they would vote for Reagan if Walter Mondale were his competition.

After the speech: 56 percent said they would vote for Reagan over Mondale.

Reagan's eventual vote tally 53 weeks later was almost exactly that number: 59 percent.

The president's approval ratings rose immediately after Grenada and he never trailed, not in the following summer after the Democratic convention, not in October following a poor performance in the first presidential debate; and certainly not in November, when he carried 49 states in demolishing Democrats Walter Mondale and Geraldine Ferraro, the first woman ever to run for national office on a major ticket.

This is particularly important when you consider that 61 percent of the people who voted for Reagan said they made up their minds before Jan. 1, less than nine weeks after his speech on Oct. 27.

Certainly the invasion of Grenada itself had the potential to stir those new, chauvinistic, patriotic feelings. But it was the speech, which linked Grenada, patriotism, and Reagan himself into one grand, intertwined symbol of strength and hope that brought the true, lasting response.

Even a year and a half after the 1984 election, almost two-thirds of the adults in the USA felt Ronald Reagan was doing a good or excellent job. Here are the results:

Generally speaking, what kind of job do you think President Reagan is doing?	
Excellent	19%
Good	42
Fair	27
Poor	11

And even though he's 75 years old, 85 percent say Reagan's age and health don't affect his performance.

Ronald Reagan is a person who confounded a lot of critics during the 1980s, and, in many ways, set the tone for the Image Age.

In 1986 we asked people to name the USA's greatest hero. We asked the question "open-ended," which means no prompting, no pre-set answers to choose from.

More than 100 different people were named, from Dallas Cowboys football coach Tom Landry to Miami Vice star Don Johnson. But No. 1 on the list was Ronald Reagan. He was named by 50 percent of all adults. To give you an idea of how overwhelming was Reagan's support, Jesse Jackson placed second. He had only 4 percent.

Let's take a look back, for a minute, to some of the reasons that Ronald Reagan won his re-election in such an over-whelming manner. Many analysts back then failed to recognize that the campaign always focused on Reagan. The election was his to win or lose. Walter Mondale was hardly a factor.

Consider these results from USA TODAY polls:

- 62 percent of those who voted for Reagan said they were doing so because they liked him, not because they disliked Mondale.
- By contrast, only 34 percent of Mondale voters said they were voting for him because they like him; half said they were voting for Mondale because they disliked Reagan.

- Even the poor, households with incomes under $10,000—a traditional Democratic stronghold—favored Reagan over Mondale.

One potential Reagan liability, his age, never became an issue.

At the beginning of the campaign 75 percent rated Reagan as good or excellent for his ability to work hard and stay vigorous, virtually the same as Mondale's rating. That confidence never wavered, even after the first Reagan-Mondale debate, Oct. 7, 1984, when the president looked tired and unsure of himself. Indeed, it held fast even though viewers, in a poll taken immediately after the debate, showed that Mondale had won a narrow victory.

Who do you think won tonight's debate:	
Mondale	39%
Reagan	34
Tie	14
Not Sure	13

Another survey, a few days later, showed Mondale winning by 10 more points. And in a testament to the power of the media, our results showed his lead larger among people who had read or heard about the debate but had not seen it for themselves.

Still, the president's debate-night fumble cost him only a temporary loss of a few points off his massive lead. Even after the debate:

- 75 percent said Reagan was not too old to handle a second term as president.
- 54 percent said he simply had an off-night during the first debate.

There was no doubt about what happened at the second presidential debate: 44 percent felt Reagan had won compared with 27 percent for Mondale.

Was it an "issues" election?

Not really, according to our polls. Voters favored Mondale's policy on some of the most critical issues facing the USA today: the environment, women's rights, and improving conditions for the poor. They even felt that Mondale would be more likely to avoid nuclear war, promote job opportunities, cut poverty, and improve conditions for minorities.

But they loved Reagan; they talked about Reagan's ability to lead the nation and to come up with new ideas, his ability to handle crises. They thought that he would be more likely than Mondale to reduce the federal deficit, control inflation, support our allies abroad, and reduce crime.

And overwhelmingly, by a ratio of two to one, they favored Reagan's ability to communicate to people.

Perhaps the most incredible thing about Reagan is the continuing large majorities of citizens who give him high marks on the job and give him their personal confidence. Six out of ten still say Reagan is doing a good job in office, almost the exact same number that voted for him in 1984.

Reagan enjoys a higher rating than any recent previous president, even higher than Dwight Eisenhower at the midpoint of his second term. There is no doubt that people admire and have confidence in the man.

But what does that mean for the future?

There's no evidence, either politically or in our surveys, to indicate that 1984 was the "realigning" election that so many had predicted it would be, an election to set the tone for the next decade just as the New Deal had done in the '30s.

There was no conservative mandate; rather, it appears more and more likely that 1984 was actually a personal victory for Ronald Reagan. Even people who identify themselves as liberals give Reagan good marks.

In many ways he was a rock of stability after Nixon, Ford, and Carter. He is a man who radiates confidence and likability, even among some of his political opponents. People were confident in Nixon's abilities, but he was a strange and distant man; Ford and Carter were likable enough, but didn't elicit a great deal of confidence.

In short, at 75, Ronald Reagan may be the nation's father figure.

Still, the people are discerning enough to separate the president from his policies.

Under Reagan the public's faith in the federal government continues to drop, and major national problems like the farm crisis and the federal budget deficit remain unsolved. People still fear nuclear war. In fact, 51 percent tell us that the president could do more to avoid war.

In fact, it is just that ability of Reagan's to separate himself from the issues around him that made his popularity so enduring. He earned the monicker "The Teflon President," for no issue could stick to him for very long.

Ethical questions abounded in his administration, but most of us feel that the the Reagan administration is no better or no worse ethically than past administrations. A strong 64 percent say Reagan aides have behaved about on par for administrations in the past 20 years.

In fact, we're more likely to blame the press: 77 percent say the media turn minor incidents in major scandals. (Most people, however, do think that high government officials should be held at a higher level of accountability than others; 71 percent favor requiring government officials to disclose investments and income.)

Take a look at one more example—perhaps the most embarrassing episode in the Reagan presidency. In 1985 the president was scheduled to a visit a World War II cemetery during a visit to West Germany. The trip created a national storm of controversy when it was revealed that Nazis were buried in the cemetery, and Reagan's visit was seen as a horrible slight to the Nazis' victims.

The scandal became so talked about that the name of the cemetery, Bitburg, became a household word. There were waves of protests and vehement calls for the president to cancel his trip. Reagan refused.

Our survey during the period showed that more than half of all USA adults were opposed to Reagan visiting the cemetery.

But who did the public blame?

Not the president. Two out of three blamed Reagan aides for "poor planning." Once again Ronald Reagan, the great communicator, the Teflon president, had worked his magic.

For all that, a president can only serve eight years; and when Ronald Reagan leaves us on Jan. 20, 1989, many issues will remain. Let's turn our attention to some of those issues.

Getting Elected

Actually, the first of those has already begun. By mid-1986 the battle for the presidency is already under way. The names have begun to surface, none declared as candidates, all considered as such: George Bush, Jack Kemp, Gary Hart, Mario Cuomo, and more.

More than two years before the next election, Ronald Reagan's term is not half done, but already the 1988 election is big copy on the USA's radio, TV, newspapers, and magazines. Is this too soon to start thinking about the next resident of 1600 Pennsylvania Avenue?

You bet it is, say the people who decide who gets to live there.

More than two-thirds of us, almost seven out of 10 adults, say the presidential campaign is just too long and should be shortened.

And three out of four, 76 percent, say that voters lose interest in the campaign because the candidates have to say the same thing over and over again to different audiences, particularly during the long primary season.

How should the primary season be shortened? Well, unfortunately, we're not nearly as united on that front.

Three alternatives were debated in 1984. We asked the public about each. Here are the results:

Proposal	Percent who agree
Stay with the current system	32%
A regional primary with several states holding primaries on the same day	29
A one-day national primary	28

National Priorities

Reducing the budget deficit and avoiding nuclear war are two of the most important problems facing the nation today, people have told us on survey after survey. This has changed since the early '80s when the economy topped the list, and the late '70s when we specifically wanted the government to deal with double-digit inflation.

But we want our money spent in places that will affect us more directly, such as improving education and cutting crime. Here are the results when we asked people to help us set our national priorities.

What are the most important problems for government to solve?

Problem	Percent citing
Reduce budget deficit	62%
Nuclear arms limitations	60
Cut crime	58
Cut unemployment	53
Control inflation	51
Environmental pollution	40
Helping the poor	37
Equal rights for men/women	26

Where are the most important places for the federal government to spend our money?

Improve education	68%
Reduce drug use	63
Reduce crime	62
Reduce unemployment	54
Improve health care	54
Social Security	51
Improve environment	47
Improve highways, bridges	41
Support farmers	39
Improve conditions for minorities	27
National defense	21
Space exploration	19
Foreign aid	11

Who's Got the Clout

Influence is everything in Washington, particularly if you can influence the voters. To find out who has the clout with the voters and who doesn't, we offered the names of a number of organizations, and asked voters: Would you be more likely to vote for a candidate because he or she was endorsed by one of these organizations? The results were somewhat surprising:

Organization	Percent favorably influenced by endorsement
National Education Association	45%
Environmentalist groups	32
Right to Life groups	27
U.S. Chamber of Commerce	25
National Organization of Women	23
AFL-CIO	21
American Federation of State, County and Municipal Employees	21
NAACP	20
Moral Majority	18

The Budget Deficit

Concern about the federal budget deficit has grown enormously during the '80s and will likely continue growing until it becomes one of our major issues—second only to nuclear war—for the rest of the decade (or, to dream for a moment, until the problem is solved).

By the mid-'80s, 88 percent of the USA adults said they were concerned about the deficit; almost nine out of 10. Over half, 51 percent said they were very concerned. Clearly, the tide of red ink flowing out of Washington will be a major issue in the 1988 election.

Ronald Reagan came into office with a promise to cut the deficit and whittle away at the national debt. Neither has occurred, yet a minority blame Reagan for the failure. We asked recently where the buck stops.

Who's responsible for the deficit?	
Congress	59%
Reagan	22
Both	11
Not sure	8

OK, we know that a vast majority of people think the deficit is dangerous, so how should we cut it?

We asked people to tell us which proposals they *oppose*, to find out where the logjam might be. Guess what? Once again, we're better at finding the problem than agreeing on a solution; we're no more united on how to cut the deficit than Congress is.

	Percent opposed
Reduce domestic spending	47%
Reduce defense spending	37
Increase taxes	34

There is one solution, however, which enjoys widespread support. More than half, 58 percent, say they favor a constitutional amendment to require a balanced budget.

The Infernal Revenue Service

The mid-'80s weren't kind to the Internal Revenue Service. Never a favorite of the people of the USA, the IRS in 1986 was late delivering millions of tax returns. There was a massive computer failure and allegations that workers actually threw away some tax returns.

Despite its problems, however, most of us think the IRS actually does a pretty good job. Almost two-thirds, 63 percent, say they're confident that the IRS accurately and quickly handles our tax returns.

In fact, you can argue that we think the IRS does a better job for us than we do for the IRS. We believe that an average of 38 percent of our friends and neighbors deliberately cheat on their taxes—more than one in three. And almost an identical number, 36 percent, say they wouldn't think badly of a friend who got caught cheating.

Here are some other observations on the tax man:

■ We fear the IRS; 57 percent say cheaters are likely to be caught.

■ Taxpayers are evenly split on whether federal income taxes are fair: 48 percent say yes; 47 percent say no.

■ More than two-thirds of us think special interest groups and the rich get special privileges under current tax laws.

- 74 percent say they believe people cheat because cheaters think the tax system is unfair to them.
- 69 percent say they would work harder if the extra income they earned were taxed less.
- 47 percent say it's fairly easy to figure out their taxes.
- Finally, one more nice note for the IRS: 64 percent say they think auditors basically try to be fair and helpful in auditing taxpayer returns. Only 19 percent disagree.

The Cost of War

The most important problem facing the USA is the serious threat of a nuclear war.

Eight out of 10 adults don't believe there will be a global nuclear war, at least not in the next 10 years. Most of us do believe, however, that we'll continue to be involved in smaller international conflicts, such as in Lebanon or Vietnam.

We believe the result of an all-out war would be doomsday, leaving a globe in ashes, totally unlivable. When we asked people to predict the outcome of a nuclear war, this is what they told us:

What happens if the Soviet Union and the USA do clash in an all-out war?	
Result	Percent
The USA wins	11%
The Soviets win	1
Russia and the USA are destroyed as places to live	30
The entire world is destroyed and unlivable	51

Once again, we are thoroughly split, as a nation, on a solution to the problem. For example: On the subject of arms reduction, the number of people saying the USA needs to be stronger than the Soviet Union is almost exactly equal to the number saying we need to be "as strong."

This is a key question for us to resolve as a nation: Arms reduction is one of the things we'd most like to see happen between the USA and the USSR, but far down the list of things we think are likely to happen. We asked: How would you like to see the USA and Soviet Union cooperate in an attempt to reduce strife and ease tensions in the world? The result:

	Percent citing	Percent saying it's likely
Arms reduction	84%	35%
Increased cultural exchange	84	68
Expanded trade	84	76
Joint space exploration	75	55
Allowing more emigration from USSR	72	18
Banning space weapons	70	30
Sharing scientific research	61	44

So there you have a glimpse of the problems and politics of the nation. The issues of the '70s and early '80s—particiularly economics and inflation—are fading. The issues of the federal deficit, arms control, and peace are emerging, and, given the history of our presidential elections, we should be hearing more and more about them in the months leading to the 1988 election.

CHAPTER FOURTEEN

General
Feelings

Well, there you have it: the USA today. Everything you could possibly want to know about what the USA says of the decade that brought you new wave music, Mr. T, Walkmans, Watchmans, Wham!, Rambo, IRAs, Cabbage Patch Kids, Gerry Ferraro, James Watt, hi-fi VCRs, and a refurbished Statue of Liberty.

Well, almost everything.

We've taken you through the Image Age; met women in conflict between desiring new goals and clinging to old ones. We've seen men who say what they want, but don't want what they say. We've seen marriage surviving and looked at what happens when one doesn't. We've gone to work with you and with some of the most successful people in the USA. We've watched people in the USA grow old, go to college, wave the flag, turn on the TV.

But what about everything else?

In the final chapter we're going to take a look at the '90s—using the USA TODAY surveys to peek into the future. But first, let's wrap up a few last random thoughts people have shared with us about the '80s. This is, in no particular order, a smorgasbord of What You Think About All Sorts of Things.

There She Is

Let's start with a national institution: the beauty contest.

From Miss Dairy Delight of Marshall County to Miss Universe, they are an inherent part of our national experience. And the prototype for all of them, in the national mind, is the Miss America pageant.

The pageant, long under attack from feminists, became the center of controversy in the '80s—putting the moral questions about these pageants back onto the front pages. There was Vanessa Williams, who resigned as Miss America after *Penthouse* magazine discovered nude photos for which she posed years earlier.

It was the most publicized scandal, but there were lesser ones: A year earlier, Miss America 1983, Debra Sue Maffett, battled reports that she'd undergone surgery to improve her breasts. Miss New Jersey Toni Georgiana had to go to court to fight charges that she didn't really live in New Jersey.

No matter how you feel about the pageant—whether it's a stepping stone for young women trying to move into modeling careers, or an exploitative symptom of an archaic sexist view of females—it's *there,* marking the passing years, like the Superbowl and Income Tax Day. Love it or hate it, there was a certain sadness when Bert Parks was fired from the Miss America pageant. Like Guy Lombardo and New Year's Eve, like Walter Cronkite and the evening news—these are experiences that become part of What This Country Is, on a level beyond whether you like them or not.

But do you like them or not?

The 65-year-old Miss America pageant is still OK in the USA's book, people told us. The results are not an overwhelming mandate in favor, but they're more pro than con.

About 50 percent don't believe that the pageant exploits women; only 37 percent say it does. In fact, 75 percent feel that the contestants exploit the competition, by using it as a stepping stone, more than the competition exploits the women. Only 19 percent disagree.

And when we asked people with daughters whether they'd want them to compete, more said yes than no: 48 percent to 40 percent.

Made in the USA

The question comes up for different reasons—sometimes

purely economic, sometimes purely patriotic—but should you look for the label that says "Made in the USA"? The push has come up often—most recently in a widespread mid-'80s TV push using high-profile celebrities from Don Johnson to Bob Hope saying, "It matters to me."

Does it matter to you?

More of you say it does than say it doesn't.

Across the nation, 54 percent of us always try to buy products that were made in the USA; 8 percent make the effort sometimes; 37 percent buy whatever appeals to them, regardless of its nation of origin.

There are some interesting breakdowns here. Union members and older people lead the support for domestic products. Among union members, 67 percent say they always buy American—probably because they are most conscious of how it affects jobs in the USA. About 50 percent of nonunion members say they won't buy non-USA products.

The age difference is striking, too: 67 percent of people over 65 say they always try to buy products made in the USA—but only 25 percent of people age 18 to 25 look for the USA label.

The Peace Corps

The Peace Corps was another national institution in the '60s, and although it's not nearly as high-profile as it once was, it's still faring pretty well in the minds of the public.

We went back to basics with this topic: The first question we wondered about was whether people even *remembered* the name of the government agency that sent so many volunteers abroad. The results were encouraging: 60 percent were immediately able to identify this group as the Peace Corps. (When we gave them a hint—"It was created during the Kennedy administration; and several thousand predominantly younger volunteers lived and worked in developing countries through the agency"—that jumped to 74 percent.)

It's obviously not as much a part of the USA experience as it used to be; 78 percent of us say we're hearing less about the Peace Corps than we used to. Nevertheless, 83 percent are aware that it's still around, and we still strongly support its efforts: 79 percent say it's important that the Peace Corps continue as it is.

We even tried something tricky. Often, one of the main complaints about overseas programs we hear from people is this: The money should be spent to help solve problems in our own country. So we asked a question we thought would play right into this chauvinism: Would you rather see that money spent in the USA?

The Peace Corps still received a strong vote of support: By a margin of 50 percent to 37 percent, people said no, keep the Peace Corps operating abroad.

Drug Testing

It became the subject of crude jokes: "Some baseball players would rather play between the white lines; some would rather snort them." It became a wide-ranging scandal: college coaches charged with distributing steroids, baseball players testifying about cocaine use in the locker room.

Drug use in sports became a major issue of the '80s, sometimes pushing the game results themselves off the front pages of newspaper sports sections. The reaction was strong, and we haven't seen the last of it.

The most common—and controversial—response to the growing drug problem in professional and college sports was the proposal to test athletes for drugs in the bloodstream. Those in favor said it was the only way to restore the public faith in athletes. "We'll be successful and eliminate drugs from baseball," Baseball Commissioner Peter Ueberroth told USA TODAY, "so that youngsters all over the United States and Canada can look properly at baseball players as their sports idols."

Those against warned that drug testing was a terribly dangerous infringement of civil rights. And sports became just the cornerstone of the argument: In 1986 a government task force recommended drug tests for goverment workers and contractors, and suggested that private industry consider following suit for employees in many walks of life.

When we asked the USA about drug testing, we found some concern that it could infringe on personal rights—but a stronger feeling that drugs are becoming a greater danger in the workplace, and that drug testing may be the answer.

We asked first about the proposal that government employees be tested, as that government committee suggested. A strong majority of the nation was in favor: 62 percent said yes, 29 percent said no. We were about split, however, on the question of whether all employees should be tested.

What is interesting is that we're in favor of drug testing despite the fact that we feel such testing is an infringement of individual rights—55 percent say it is; only 37 percent say it isn't. In fact, an overwhelming 77 percent say they themselves wouldn't mind being tested.

The breakdown by age groups shows a growing concern by young adults about drug use. People age 18 to 24 are by far the most likely to call drug testing a violation of individual rights; 71 percent feel that way. But they are close to older people, those 45 and over, in their strong support for drug testing.

Clearly, athletes have been the focus of the drug scandals of the 1980s, but they are not the focus of the nation's attention when we think about drug problems. A modest 51 percent say we should be tougher on athletes because they are role models for children; 45 percent disagreed with that idea. And when we asked simply, "Should we be tougher on professional athletes than anyone else who uses drugs?" 65 percent said no.

Given a wide range of employees, which do we feel should be tested for drugs and which shouldn't? Athletes came out in the middle of the pack—somewhere below school bus drivers and pilots, who topped the list, but above rock stars and other entertainers, whom we felt least strongly about testing for drugs.

Here are the professions we listed and the percentage of people saying they should be subjected to drug testing:

Profession	Percent of pubic saying those professionals should be tested for drugs
School bus drivers	86%
Airline pilots	86
Police officers	83
Firefighters	80
Nurses	79
Doctors/Dentists	79

Railroad employees	78
Teachers	77
Truck drivers	77
Federal government workers	65
Pro athletes	64
Lawyers	57
Factory workers	53
Bank tellers	52
Rock stars	44
Other entertainers	41

When we asked specifically if people favor drug testing for college athletes, 69 percent said yes; for high school athletes, 65 percent were in favor.

We don't, however, favor extremely strict punishments—we feel warnings and rehabilitation are more in order for first-offenders. Here's what we think should happen to people who are tested positive for drugs for the first time (the answers add up to more than 100 percent, since people could offer more than one answer):

Punishment	Percent in favor
Warning	91%
Ordered to enter rehabilitation program	53
Fine	38
Temporary suspension from job	27
Offender turned over to police	24
Firing	5

Disasters in the Sky

It's an important trend to keep an eye on as we move into the 1990s: When the USA is involved in tragedy, the people of our nation strongly rally around the president and the country.

Always be careful when you read these polls: People's initial reaction often changes as time goes by. For example, after a major plane crash, people tend to say they'll fly less, but overall these disasters don't really decrease the number of people traveling by plane.

What these surveys do show us is people's concern for the nation, their pride in it. And nowhere has this pride shone through as strongly as after the explosion of the space shuttle Challenger.

In January of 1986, the shuttle, with seven people aboard, including teacher Christa McAuliffe, exploded 72 seconds after launch. It was a tragedy the likes of which the nation had rarely experienced because so many millions watched it live on television, and lived through it first-hand.

As a result the nation's grief was heartfelt and immediate, deep and personal. And out of that grief has sprung a support for a space program that, in recent years, had become almost routine, attracting less and less of the public's attention.

You might think that after such a disaster, especially one that was experienced so personally by so many, the natural reaction—even if only a temporary one—would be to suggest a curtailment or at least a reduction of the shuttle program.

The result was exactly the opposite. People rallied behind NASA and argued strongly for resuming the program— assuming that NASA could find the problem and fix it. A solid 73 percent of the nation was in favor. Only 5 percent felt it should be ended; 16 percent said it should be cut back.

The support was consistent—among all age groups, among people of all educational levels (although college graduates in particular backed the program's resumption). The West was strongest in favor, the South least, but all geographic regions said let the program continue.

The support was greatest among men; 81 percent said the schedule should be resumed. Among women, 66 percent said keep it flying, 20 percent favored a cutback, and 8 percent said end it altogether.

It was similar to shifts the nation took after all sorts of disasters. When the Soviet Union downed a Korean airliner, for example, President Reagan gained support across the USA for more defense spending, weapons buildups, and sanctions against the Soviets. In fact, 23 percent said the incident increased their support for Reagan himself.

After the shuttle explosion, in a response that seemed almost a memorial to Christa McAuliffe, the same 73 percent said civilians should continue to be part of the space shuttle program. Again, men were more strongly in favor than women, but the support came from across the board—all age groups, all education levels, all regions of the country.

However, when we asked, "If you yourself were offered the opportunity to go on the shuttle, would you do it?"—the response was negative. Only 18-to-24-year-olds gave more yesses than noes; overall, the nation said no by 56 percent to 40 percent.

Because there was a schoolteacher aboard, the shuttle mission attracted a great deal of attention in schools. Many students watched the explosion while it happened. Psychologists said children would have many questions about the disaster, from why it happened to who would take care of the astronauts' children.

But the nation wasn't sure whether it wanted to deal with the problem in that way. Among people with children, about half talked to their kids about it, and about half didn't.

Of those who did, the two main topics of conversation were an attempt to explain the tragedy—what death means—and an attempt to explain to the children that striving for achievement involves risk.

Spare the Rod, Please

The margin isn't wide enough to make a schoolchild feel comfortable, but 51 percent say kids should not be spanked if they misbehave in school; 46 percent say they should; 3 percent aren't sure.

Take Me Out to Seven Ballgames

For some, the most important change of the '80s had nothing to do with women in the workplace, AIDS, crime, or the divorce rate: The nation was split over how it felt about extending the baseball playoffs.

The year 1986 became the year that the American League and National League Championship series were changed from best-of-five to best-of-seven. By a probably insignificant four percentage points, the USA gave a whisper of an OK to this change—45 percent were in favor, 41 percent against.

Interestingly, women liked it better than men did. Women were 45-to-34 in favor—with a big 21 percent undecided—while men were 47-to-45 against. Fans in the Northeast were the most enthusiastic.

Said a fan in favor: "My wife and I are senior citizens, and for selfish reasons we want to see more games televised." Said a fan against: "A lot of times there are programs I like to watch at night, like *Dallas*, and you can't see them because sports are on instead. There's too much sports on TV at night as it is. Who needs more?"

By the way, lots of us need more, although the national pastime isn't the nation's favorite. More people say they're fans of football—both professional and college—than say they're followers of the Boys of Summer. The only sport on the list with more female fans than male: tennis.

Question: Are you a fan of the following sport?

Sport	Total	Men	Women
Pro football	54%	67%	43%
College football	45	54	37
Baseball	41	44	38
College basketball	40	46	35
Pro basketball	34	36	33
Tennis	27	26	28
Golf	21	24	18
Pro hockey	15	18	13

Feeling Safe

Women in the USA feel much less safe than men do.

- Sixty-three percent of us feel "very safe" in our homes alone at night—73 percent of men, 53 percent of women.
- 39 percent of women feel unsafe traveling after dark on public transportation, compared to 21 percent of men.
- 13 percent of women fear going to the store at night by car, more than twice as much as men do.
- Three times as many women as men feel unsafe walking alone in their neighborhood at night.

Lawyers

In Shakespeare's *Henry VI, Part 2*, a group of commoners are fantasizing about what they'll do when one of their ranks becomes king: "The first thing we do," says Dick the

Butcher, "let's kill all the lawyers."

Well, the USA isn't quite that angry at the members of the legal profession. In fact, we give them high marks for ethics and hard work. But overall, we feel there are too many lawyers filing too many lawsuits and getting paid too much money for them.

And in many ways, the USA's lawyers agree: "There's too damn many attorneys coming out and finding too damn many things to litigate," a Kansas lawyer told us.

We did two separate polls—one of the USA public, one of the nation's lawyers—to find out how we felt about what is becoming an increasingly litigious society.

The polls showed a public getting more and more fed up with the legal system, and many lawyers feeling pretty much the same way.

For starters, here's how we feel about lawyers:

- 80 percent of the public (and 72 percent of lawyers) say that too many civil cases are filed that shouldn't be going to court in the first place; 79 percent say it's too easy to sue, and 70 percent feel lawyers are too anxious to sue.
- 28 percent of people who hired a lawyer in the past two years say they wouldn't go back to the same lawyer.
- 56 percent of us feel that lawyers recommend more legal work than is actually required, because it increases their fees; 35 percent disagree.
- 73 percent say that because there are too many lawyers, many disputes are being taken to court when they shouldn't be. Only 19 percent disagree.
- Are lawyer's fees generally reasonable? sixty-one percent say yes; 29 percent say no.

But we do have some nice things to say about lawyers. A majority feel that lawyers follow high legal standards (64 percent say they do; 28 percent say they don't).

A bigger majority feels that lawyers generally work hard to protect the interests of their clients (71 percent say they do; 21 percent say they don't).

Why are so many disputes clogging up the court system?
Well, 68 percent of lawyers admit that some people in their own profession are just too eager to sue. But they see other

reasons as well: 64 percent say people in the USA are better informed about their own rights. And about half feel that society has become filled with more conflict—and more of those conflicts must be settled in court.

The public at large doesn't see eye-to-eye with its lawyers, however, when it comes to solutions to the problem.

Plea bargaining—getting a defendant to plead guilty to a lesser charge in exchange for dropping more serious charges—is one way that the legal system keeps cases from tying up the courts. But we're wary of that as a solution: 72 percent of us say that plea bargaining should be reserved for the less serious cases. Only 14 percent of lawyers agree.

And 72 percent of us feel that lawyers should be disciplined for filing "frivolous" lawsuits; only 47 percent of lawyers feel the same way.

Two other solutions offered: 61 percent of lawyers think judges should dismiss more cases; 70 percent of the public likes the idea of having people who sue and lose pay the legal fees of the person they sued.

When do people really need a lawyer? We asked the lawyers to tell us. Here are seven circumstances, and the percentage of lawyers saying you should contact a lawyer when they happen:

	Need a lawyer	Don't need a lawyer
Defending a drunk-driving charge	94%	4%
Drawing up a will	93	5
Settling a real estate purchase	84	11
Settling a no-fault divorce	84	11
Settling neighborhood dispute, such as a dog-bite case:	35	45
Challenging a minor traffic citation	13	75
Renting an apartment	11	79

And when you do need a lawyer, what's the best way to find one?

Of the lawyers surveyed, 68 percent said "ask a friend or relative for a reference"; 25 percent recommended calling your local bar association; 2 percent suggested the Yellow Pages.

Only one in a hundred recommended looking at those new legal-service advertisements.

The survey of lawyers also revealed some interesting insights into their profession. Among the things we found:

- The average hourly rate for lawyers we polled: $88.52.
- Some take a percentage of what you win in a lawsuit. The average: 32 percent.
- About half think legal costs are "about right"; 34 percent say they're too high, 12 percent say too low.
- How can the poor get legal help? Thirty-five percent favor prepaid legal insurance; 33 percent favor volunteer help; 29 percent favor government-subsidized legal services; and 22 percent favor low-cost legal clinics.

Nobody Knows the Troubles I've Seen

Here are the things we consider our most frequent problems:

Family finances	25%
Health	13
Job	9
Social life	9
Marriage	6
Children	6
Sex life	6

On the flip side, here are the parts of our lives we think are improving:

Family life	43%
Finances	40
Job	33
Social life	29
Sex life	25
Health	18

And to check in once more with our poll of almost 1,000 mental health workers, psychologists, and psychiatrists: 68 percent say their patients' problems stem from things that happened (or didn't happen) in their childhood; and 66 percent think reading self-help books generally is helpful to people (only 5 percent think they do more harm than good).

Secret Killers

One of the strangest phenomena that began to surface in the 1980s, one that we can only pray will not become a continuing part of the national scene, was the apparently random act of violence committed by people tampering with products on store shelves.

While a variety of products had to deal with tampering scares—even Girl Scout cookies weren't immune—the problem seemed to center on drugs sold in capsules. After the latest wave of these poisonings, in early 1986—cyanide found in Tylenol capsules—we asked people what they thought.

People in the USA don't seem ready to let these random tamperings dictate the way we live our lives, even in small ways. A majority say they'll still use over-the-counter capsules. About three out of four say Tylenol's manufacturer was right to put the capsules back on the market, after trying to make them more tamper-resistant following the first poisonings. We were two to one against a government ban on over-the-counter sales of medicines sold in capsules; and we expressed confidence in tamper-resistant packages by more than three to one.

Up on the Farm

As we mentioned awhile back, farmers in the USA are suffering from what many say is the worst farm crisis since the Depression.

In mid-decade, the USA began waking up to the terrible magnitude of the problem. Once again, the popular media were enlisted to get people's attention. Movies such as *The River* and *Country* dramatized the farmer's plight; in the spirit of Band Aid and USA for Africa, country singers held a massive Farm Aid concert to focus attention on the problem. Dan Rather even anchored the evening news from the farm belt for a week, visiting farmers in trouble and sitting in on family-style suppers.

As the government struggled with tough questions over

farm bills and prices, farmers fought a growing wave of fore-closures.

In the midst of all this, the people across the USA gave a rousing vote of support for the farmer. Some politicians felt that farming is a business that doesn't deserve federal support any more than any other business, but the people disagreed. A firm 71 percent say the federal government has an obligation to give financial help to troubled farmers. Only 22 percent disagreed.

Even when it came to their own pocketbooks, people showed support for farmers. The Agriculture Department says Americans spend about 15 percent of their take-home pay on food, down from 20 percent in 1960. When we asked people about food prices, 61 percent said what they pay for food is just about right; only half as many said prices are too high.

We're not as strongly in favor of the government going so far as to guarantee minimum prices for farmers: 48 percent think that's a good idea, but 35 percent think the marketplace should determine prices, even if it means that some farmers will go out of business.

But the strongest feelings came out when we asked, "Do farmers represent an important way of life that needs the financial support of the federal government?" Across the USA, 76 percent of us said yes; only 19 percent said no.

Doctors

A few pages back we took a look at what the USA thinks of its lawyers, and what lawyers think of themselves.

Now let's do the same with doctors.

One thing we agree on with our doctors (in fact, one of the few things we agree on) is that medical costs are too high. Among doctors, 65 percent say they're too high, but 55 percent planned to raise their own fees in the coming year. The average increase planned: 9.3 percent.

The biggest promised rate hikes came from doctors practicing in urban areas, from psychiatrists, and from gynecologists.

This will be a key issue to watch as the decade winds down.

The problem of soaring malpractice insurance costs has become so severe that some doctors have reportedly refused to treat certain patients, and thousands of doctors have staged mass rallies to protest. It is certain to have an effect on how doctors run their practices (and, most likely, on how much it costs us to see them).

How much do doctors earn? Here's what a national cross-section of doctors we surveyed told us:

Less than $40,000	8%
$41,000 to $75,000	34
$76,000 to $100,000	29
$101,000 to $150,000	20
$151,000 to $200,000	5
More than $200,000	4

Doctors and their patients disagree about a number of things we asked about. For example, we wait in their offices longer than they think we do; and we feel closer to them than they think we do.

First, look at the amount of time doctors think we spend out there among the month-old magazines, and how long we say we spend waiting out there (note particularly the first and last lines on this chart):

Waiting time	Doctors say	Patients say
Less than 10 minutes	28%	10%
10-15 minutes	33	23
15-20 minutes	19	24
20-25 minutes	13	18
More than 30 minutes	4	20

When we asked if doctors' relationships with their patients have grown closer or more distant over the past year, the differences between what we said and what the doctors said were significant. We are twice as likely as our doctors to say we're getting closer:

	Doctors say	Patients say
Closer	12%	24%

More distant	52	8
The same	31	67

This came through in another way, too: A vast majority of us—74 percent—say doctors routinely take the time to patiently answer questions about treatment and diagnosis. A change that seems to be emerging in that relationship is this: People seem to be trying to become more involved in their own treatment. More than eight out of 10 doctors say patients are more likely than they used to be to ask questions about the doctor's diagnosis. We say the same, although not in as large numbers: 52 percent of us say we question the doctor more than in years past; 41 percent say we simply accept the doctor's diagnosis.

One more thing we seem to disagree about: how often we should go see the doctor. About 36 percent of doctors, including 50 percent of pediatricians, say people see doctors too often.

We seem to be less comfortable in our relationships with hospitals. While 83 percent say hospitals provide better-than-adequate care, our biggest complaints: High fees topped the list, followed by the feeling that poor management results in poor care (and in higher costs).

A few more things that doctors had to say about us:

- 57 percent of the doctors say patients are suffering from more stress-related illnesses now than just a few years ago. Gynecologists are most likely to blame stress for a growing number of ailments. (This jibes with what the psychologists told us: Remember, 91 percent of them say stress in the workplace and home contribute significantly to psychological problems in the 1980s.)
- 67 percent of the doctors say patients take too many over-the-counter drugs.
- While there is little change in how frequently doctors themselves prescribe drugs, 60 percent say they are ordering more medical tests now than a decade ago.

And now a few things doctors say about themselves. For one thing, most of them agree that there are too many doctors in their own community. But there's a big difference depending on what community you're talking about, and the differences underscore a serious need for more doctors in some rural areas.

Doctors: Are there too many doctors in your community?

	Total	Urban	Suburban	Rural
Yes	54%	63%	55%	32%
No	37	28	34	64

- 66 percent of the doctors say that if they had it to do over again, they would still become doctors; 14 percent say no, and 20 percent aren't sure.
- As we mentioned earlier, only 30 percent of doctors say they want their children to be doctors; 33 percent say they don't want their kids to follow in their footsteps (the rest didn't care or weren't sure). Gynecologists were the least likely to want their own children to become doctors; psychiatrists were the most likely.
- 38 percent say they know of doctors who knowingly perform unnecessary treatment on patients; 50 percent say they don't.
- A whopping 89 percent of doctors complain that medical schools didn't prepare them for the business of running a practice.
- 72 percent say Americans trained in medical schools outside the USA are not as qualified as doctors trained in this country.

The Right to Die

A final point on medical care, and one that has become the center of one of the most difficult moral issues of our time.

Technology in the medical field is advancing much faster than our ability to make clear choices about how, and when, and whether to use that technology. Doctors can now keep patients alive through extraordinary means. But whether they should do so and whether the quality of life that results should be considered a factor in deciding treatment are questions at the center of a debate that has only begun to rage. And this issue is certain to get more difficult, and more morally confusing, as technology and medical breakthroughs continue to advance.

The issue, in the popular press, began to be called "The Right to Die." It took on many, many forms, and none of the answers was easy.

Elizabeth Bouvia, a cerebral palsy patient, wanted a California hospital to let her starve to death; she saw it as a matter of "refusing treatment," but while she was staying there the hospital force-fed her. In another case, the parents of a severely handicapped infant identified only as "Baby Jane Doe" fought attempts to force on them surgery that would prolong her life.

Our survey showed that people feel strongly that dying patients and their families have the right to withhold or halt life-sustaining medical treatment. Almost three out of four, 73 percent, believe the patient has that right, even if it means certain death. And 65 percent say that a doctor should be allowed to stop treating an unconscious terminally ill patient if asked to do so by the patient's family.

In the last chapter we'll pull together some of the trends and attitudes we've discussed and take a look at the future.

CHAPTER FIFTEEN

A Look
at the Future

The year was 1900. The nation was agog at moving into a new century, thrilled at the promise of what the future would bring. *Ladies' Home Journal* called on a man named John Elfreth Watkins, Jr., to write about what life would be like in the next 100 years. Watkins predicted that:

- Coal won't be used for heating or cooking. (He was pretty much right on that one.)
- Mail will be delivered through giant tubes. (Wrong, though sometimes we wish someone would explore the idea.)
- Hot and cold air will be controlled by spigots. (Not bad; we call them thermostats, though.)
- Automobiles will be cheaper than workhorses. (Wrong!)
- Trains will travel 150 mph. (Right!)
- Man will see around the world with giant screens. (Right again; we call them televisions.)
- Fewer drugs will be swallowed. (No comment.)

It's a tricky business, forecasting the future. So we offer this disclaimer from the start. As we have throughout this book, we're going to take a look at the trends of today—the things *you've* told us about how you live your lives—and see what they tell us about the USA of tomorrow. But keep in mind: What we offer is not a prediction of the future but rather—based on the thousands of interviews on which this book is set—what we intend the future to be.

This is where you are taking the country; this is your direction.

The trends we've encountered in our travels, some of them still barely visible today, are slowly shaping the nation that we'll live in a decade, two decades, even a generation from now. Molded by the attitudes we've explored in this book, shaped by the demands of the '80s, and propelled by our accelerating technology, the USA in the next decade will be a bigger, wealthier, healthier, more tolerant country with greater opportunity for whites and minorities alike.

It will be a nation whose men and women finally learn to work in concert, in harmony—in the home and on the job. And the satisfaction both receive from their lives is not diminished, but expanded; not cheapened, but deepened.

Certainly, there are major problems facing us in the years ahead. We can't forget about poverty, hunger, overcrowding, pollution, acid rain, intolerance, and most seriously the real threat of nuclear war. We humans have a tremendous capacity to screw up. But we have a capacity just as big to fix what we've screwed up.

There are things we know fairly well about the future, positive trends that seem solidly entrenched:

- Life expectancy has been rising, not only in the USA but throughout the world.
- Revolutions in medical care are not only allowing us to live longer, but also enabling us to live better. Every day in the USA, people who 10 years ago would have been deaf can hear. They see, where just 10 years they would have been blind. They walk, have children, and laugh, when just recently they would have been crippled, barren, in pain.
- Fears of overcrowding have eased somewhat because the birthrate is falling in the USA and in many places around the world.
- Industrialized nations have begun cleaning up their act to restore the environment. There are daily signs of hope: states banding together to clean up the Chesapeake Bay, cities fighting unsafe dump sites, legislation passing to safely remove asbestos from buildings, countries joining to solve the problem of acid rain. We have not, by any stretch

of the imagination, begun to solve all our problems, but there are growing signs of care and hope. Those who wish to protect the planet are regaining their voice.

There are monumental questions to confront.

What will become of us when we get old? By 2029, 65 million people in the nation will be senior citizens. That's 21 percent of the entire population, up from 11 percent in the mid-'80s. The number of people over the age of 85 will almost triple by 2014. The medical miracles that have extended life and make it more comfortable will also carry a staggering price tag. Who will pay this price?

Experts predict a savings surge as baby boomers mature and start worrying about Social Security. But health care will become a much greater issue over the coming decades, and it's not clear at all how we'll deal with that issue.

There's also a question of the federal budget deficit. This is a problem that *must* be faced and defeated if we are to prosper.

While many of us are celebrating the lower gas prices, others are warning that they are really setting the stage for gas shortages the likes of which we haven't seen since the early '70s. Indeed, it is true that we are driving more and that oil exploration has dried up due to the low prices.

And, most sobering of all, will we have a future in which to worry about these troubles? As we've seen, most of us don't think we'll destroy ourselves with nuclear war. Less clear to us as a nation is whether we'll cut and bleed from little skirmishes around the globe.

We don't intend to make exotic forecasts about colonies in space and the discovery of a fountain of youth that will preserve life and health for a hundred years. We're not even sure we can guess how we're going to be delivering mail 100 years from now (although we'd probably say by computer).

What we will do is look at the attitudinal, technological, and demographic trends we've been discussing thoughout this book, and see what they tell us about the possibilities for the USA in the decades to come.

A Peek at the Future

The 1980s have been a turning point. A time of tremendous

changes, hurtling toward us at machine-gun speed, forever altering the USA and its people. We are now in the process of sorting through all those changes, taking the good and discarding the ones that don't fit our lives, to build a new national spirit.

As we've seen, we're trying to separate image from reality to forge the lifestyle of the '90s. Based on what we've heard from people across the USA, here's what the nation looks like in the 1990s:

■ Individualism, personalization, and nonconformity become more accepted at home and on the job.

■ The family, after 200 years, really does become more of a partnership between men and women than at any time in our history. Women make tremendous strides in the workplace, and so do men in the home. There is a new spirit of sharing never before experienced.

■ We really are enjoying a higher standard of living, just as the college students predicted back in the 1980s. Computers and robots have boosted incomes because people can do more work in less time. The young and middle-aged can afford a nicer home, a bigger car, a better college.

■ More of us live in the suburbs, where many of the young adults of the '80s grew up.

Demographic shifts make certain industries boom in the 1990s:

■ Restaurants, because of the number of working wives and singles, increase in number and financial strength.

■ Children's products, at least through the first half of the 1990s, do very well. Then industries that cater to teens will start to soar (maybe those video parlors will come back in style!).

■ Transportation, leisure, motels, and travel industries— already growing back in the 1980s—really take off in the 1990s and beyond.

■ The medical-care industry explodes, particularly after the year 2000. Although they will be the USA's healthiest generation of elderly, and certainly the largest, older people still see doctors, visit hospitals, and use medication more than other adults. After the year 2010 nursing homes may well be a huge growth industry.

■ Recreation, a $150 billion business in the 1980s, continues to grow. One reason: the growing number of elderly people who are generally more concerned about keeping fit than are younger people and who have more time.

- Homes: It's likely that the market for second homes may increase because people have more income, better health, and more years to enjoy. That is, of course, unless the government changes the tax system, making it more costly to own a second home. Then all bets are off.

- Professional and business services: Financial services, information processing and factory automation become key industries. We move rapidly toward an information-based economy. Firms hire engineers, lawyers, public relations agents and accountants as consultants, rather than keep them on staff full time, to hold down costs.

That's the quick peek at the 1990s. Now let's look at some of the major trends in more detail.

The Family

The family is not dying, not by any stretch of the imagination. The ideas of home, work, and respect remain alive and well today and will continue to do so.

We're simply moving into a society without one single approved lifestyle model for everyone to follow. Rather, there are many models: the traditional family in which the wife stays home, two-career couples, singles, childless couples, and live-ins.

Certainly, the stereotypical couple in which neither partner has been married before is no longer the rule. But the deeper values, the love for a child or the need for a relationship with another adult, remain strong. These are what give us the most satisfaction with our lives.

Men and women are surely moving toward shared goals for career and family life. Young men and women seem ready to embrace a new way of looking at their partners in life, sharing responsibilities and goals. This should mean that young couples in the '90s are not bothered as much by the sex identity problems that affect women and men so much today.

Almost nine out of 10 women tell us they want to have children. And it's likely that more of these women than ever before will have their children without the benefit of matrimony. As our findings show, there is growing acceptance that it's OK for women to have children even if they aren't married. And what about sex?

If we were writing this chapter a year ago we would say that almost surely, men and women would be more sexually liberal. After all, a growing number of teens are sexually active and one out of four of today's college students have had a live-in relationship with someone of the opposite sex.

Now, however, we're not so sure.

The scare over AIDS has caused the USA to re-examine its sexual habits the way nothing before has. This deadly disease has had its greatest impact in the gay community, but is in no way limited to homosexuals. A third of all adults say men and women should curtail casual sex to stop the spread of the dreaded disease.

Women will grow increasingly independent, partly a natural outgrowth of the changes we've seen, partly a natural reaction to the changes we will see. Women can also expect to live an increasing share of their lives alone. This is because they will marry later, they will still outlive men, and the divorce rates will likely still remain high.

This makes it even more important that they understand the importance of being able to support themselves financially and emotionally.

By the year 2000 there will be many more two-income households in the USA and a greater sharing of family responsibilities between men and women, just what the young people of today tell us they crave.

Perhaps the biggest change we see in the last part of the 20th century and beyond is the large number of people who are elderly, or getting older, and are single. It's a phenomenon we don't hear much about now but one that will be as common a topic on those ubiquitous TV talk shows as aerobics and premenstrual syndrome are today.

Aging

If you're retiring in 2014, you're not as likely to quit working as you are to embark on a new career. The exercise and dieting you've started in your youth along with improvements in nutrition and medical research have left you in better shape for your senior years. So if you're a man you can look forward to living well into your mid-70s; longer for women.

Because the pool of younger workers is shrinking drastically, companies will be encouraging older employees to stay on the job even if it means working only part time or requires expensive retraining. This is a sharp turnabout from today when early retirement is part of the grease that keeps industry running.

By the end of the century, 100,000 people in the USA will be older than 100. And the fastest-growing age group in the country is those 85 and older.

The elderly now account for 33 percent of all health-related spending. By 2025 the number of older elderly will double.

Race

One of the biggest changes in your neighborhood, church, school, and workplace in the 1990s is the variety of people you find there.

By 2014, the percentage of Hispanics has already doubled, the proportion of Asians has more than doubled, and the percentage of whites has dropped from 80 percent to 70 percent—thanks largely to the fact that they're having smaller families.

The racial changes affect politics as well as personal lives. Many of the voters who resist minority candidates are gone. Race becomes less of an issue in political campaigns.

Work

The technology developed and enjoyed in the '80s has already swept away many jobs, created new ones and forever changed the way we work and live.

In the 1990s, dull, boring, repetitious tasks are taken care of by robots. This is not a Buck Rogers prediction; the robots started taking over some of those boring, repetitious tasks in the 1980s.

A tool-and-die maker loses his job to industrial computer equipment. But he is retrained to program the robot, just as fellow workers are retrained to run it.

Warehouse workers are replaced by robots that can fill and empty shelves on computer command. Some large industries are already using robots, in steel plants and in assembly lines. In another few years you have robots assembling robots.

For some people in the '90s, "going to work" is as easy as walking into the family room and sitting down at the home computer. Many who work at home are working for themselves to escape the competition and frustration of large companies. Thanks to technology, people can contract for work wherever they want.

If you're self employed in the '90s, you probably have a job in the fast-growing information or business or financial services industries, providing analysis and support to business and individuals in ways machines can't.

Offices are not as centralized. Corporate officers can confer by two-way television. Support staff can work from home or satellite offices on computers.

With such swift changes afoot, much of what you do becomes outdated in just a few years. Training and retraining for the job become as much a part of work as showing up—perhaps as often as each decade.

A back-to-school trend that began in the '80s—with 4.5 million adults over 25 in college full or part time, up 72 percent from a decade earlier—really takes off in the '90s.

People are used to the idea that they may have to change jobs several times in their lifetimes. USA businesses in 1985 spent about $30 billion a year on retraining, double the amount of the mid-'70s, according to the American Society for Training and Development.

What else happens in the workplace in the 1990s? Blue collar workers constitute only 10 percent of the work force by the end of the century. Smokestack industries fall rapidly, also cutting the clout of unions.

As you may recall from our chapter on college students, unions were already being held in lower esteem than in previous years. Their hold on diminishing industries furthers their decline.

Service industries continue to grow along with the information revolution. We see breakthroughs in biotechnology, the development of new materials, and new methods of protecting the environment and conserving energy.

The entrepreneur continues to be the USA's secret weapon, the fuel that powers the machine. Self-employment continues to rise in the USA through the '90s, increasing productivity and creating jobs in fields unheard of a decade ago. This will also continue to be an avenue of success for women and minority groups, leapfrogging around the bureaucracies that have grown up in some major corporations.

Perhaps the most significant change in the workplace in the 1990s is the way that companies (at least the successful ones) treat their employees. More companies in the '90s encourage creative people by taking into account their idiosyncracies and allowing them to work how and where they are most productive. This is all part of the movement away from an industrialized society where so many workers depend on the presence of others.

Some other points about the workplace in the 1990s:

- The fabled baby boom generation has reached full adulthood. Many have already been absorbed into the workplace and are approaching the age where they make important purchases and investments. At the same time, the number of new job-seekers is dropping.
- The changing shape of the population points to lower unemployment rates and a strong demand for many consumer goods and services. For several years in the '90s there are more jobs than job-seekers.
- The growing number of two-career families makes it harder for companies to persuade employees to accept transfers. Firms find that they have to offer new types of benefits to encourage their most promising people to move out and up.
- For the same reasons, the demand for child care facilities grows greatly in the 1990s, although it should cool off after the year 2000.

The Sexes

The '90s woman does not *have* to be Superwoman, nor does she have to give up her job or her family life, both so critical to her self-satisfaction.

While women were the impetus for change in the '80s, it's likely that men become responsible for completing this change in the 1990s as they continue adjusting to the tremendous social changes which are occurring around them. As women sort out the conflicting feelings that in the '80s made them try to do *everything*, men sort out the conflicting feelings that made them confused about their roles in society. The new ground broken in the '70s and '80s becomes more comfortable turf in the '90s. Role models emerge (they always do), role models that were seriously lacking in the '80s.

The '90s man and the '90s woman enter a period of more shared responsibility, particularly around the home. Women are more likely to let it go; men are more willing to pick up the slack. Men fear less the appearance of losing their masculinity, and gain the mutually supportive relationship they say they've wanted all along.

Also in the Years Ahead . . .

EDUCATION: The number of schoolchildren rises 4.9 million by the year 2000. The number of kids age 10 to 14 increases by 16 percent. Many communities have to build new schools and hire new teachers. It requires money to persuade college students, who have been shying away from teaching because of poor pay, to go back to the classroom.

MARKETING: Mass marketing becomes passé—a trend we saw beginning in the 1980s. New electronic techniques cross-reference computer data bases, allowing marketers to aim for specific, tiny groups of customers through demographic targeting. Want to send your clothing catalog only to young women who subscribe to one magazine, shop in a specific store, and have a special credit card? Finding a list including only such women is a snap in the '90s. In fact, political parties in the 1980s began using just such marketing techniques to reach the largest number of potential voters at the least possible cost.

HIGH TECHNOLOGY: The computer industry experiences a resurgence in the 1990s, because manufacturers stop trying to sell technology and discover that they've got to sell value to the customer.

The computer becomes more incorporated into everyday life. No longer do manufacturers expect people to build their lives around the machine. We see the computer and the telephone begin to merge, and yet become simpler to use without difficult languages or instructions to memorize. Using the computer becomes as easy as—well, as dialing a phone.

CRIME: Crime continues to drop in the late '80s and early 1990s, mainly because the number of teenagers decreases. It may rise again slightly, however, as the new century begins and the number of people in their late teens begins to soar.

GROWTH: Most of the USA growth continues to be in the South and West, with California the biggest gainer. We also continue moving to the suburbs (the only thing that can stop this is a significant problem with oil shortages. Huge superburbs keep popping up around the nation.

We continue to be more mobile, with two-thirds of us living in communities we weren't born in and almost half of that group living at least a five-hour car ride away.

Why This Is So

This has been, in many ways, a very rosy picture of what the USA has in store. There is one underlying factor that makes it so. The predictions have at their core the beliefs and feelings of the people in the USA today.

And at the heart of those beliefs is the undying, unflagging optimism we have sensed in the years of gathering your thoughts and opinions and desires and wants and needs.

It is there in the belief that life will be better for your children than it is for you. It is there in the fact that most people believe nuclear war will be avoided.

Now you can make the case that such a belief is not only myopic but dangerous, that it keeps us from fighting for the safeguards that ensure peace. Or you can make the case that such a belief becomes self-fulfilling, that people's lives follow their own expectations, and collectively, a nation's life follows its expectations.

We have listened to the USA speak, and we hear in that voice the strong, brave sound of emergence, of exploration, of hope. It is the voice that calls the shots; and out of that strength, out of that bravery, out of that exploration, out of that hope will come the world in which we live. The world we've talked about briefly in these last few pages is the world the USA has told us it intends to forge as we move toward the 21st century. And something in that voice tells us we have no intention of letting anything get in our way.

Index